GARDENS THAT CAN SAVE THE WORLD

GARDENS THAT CAN SAVE THE WORLD

Lottie
Delamain

Foreword by
Isabella Tree

With over 350 illustrations

TART SMALL · THINK BIG · BE AMBITIOUS · USE EVE
ORNER · ENJOY MISTAKES · RETROFIT · LOOK UP · I
ATURE · THINK CONTEXT · GROW MORE · EMPATH
· DIG DEEP · WORK TOGETHER · IMPROVE ACCESS
EMOCRATIZE · ECHO HISTORY · LOOK OUTSIDE · O
RST · REPLICATE HOME · CHOOSE CAREFULLY · REI
ATERIALS · BE SELF-SUFFICIENT · BUILD SUSTAINA
HARVEST WATER · RECYCLE AND REUSE · WASTE N
ONSERVE ENERGY · ADAPT THE EXISTING · MINE T
CHALLENGE NORMS · IGNORE OBSTACLES · RETRE
VORK TOGETHER · PLAN AHEAD · BE PATIENT · GET
BSERVE · TAKE A BREATH · READ DEEPLY · ASK QUE
MAKE A MESS · COMPOST · RECLAIM MATERIALS ·
MALL · THINK BIG · BE AMBITIOUS · USE EVERY CO
NJOY MISTAKES · RETROFIT · LOOK UP · IMITATE NA
THINK CONTEXT · GROW MORE · EMPATHIZE · DIG
WORK TOGETHER · IMPROVE ACCESS · DEMOCRAT
CHO HISTORY · LOOK OUT · OTHERS FIRST · REPLIC
OME · CHOOSE CAREFULLY · REIM CINE MATERIA

CONTENTS

Foreword   6
Introduction   8
How to use this book   10

REPAIR   18

Sue Stuart-Smith   36
Fernanda Rionda   60

EMPOWER   70

Bridget Elworthy
and Henrietta Courtauld   86
Kalpana Arias   96

NOURISH   112

Rebecca McMackin   130
John Little   144

HEAL   158

Nigel Dunnett   176
Yun Hye Hwang   188

REIMAGINE   198

David Godshall   218
Elise Van Middelem   232

Glossary   244
Bibliography   250
Acknowledgments   251
Picture credits   252
Index   253

Foreword

In 2022 in Montreal, Canada, 196 countries reached a momentous decision: to preserve the life-support systems on which every species – including our own – depends. The Global Biodiversity Agreement pledges to reverse the loss of nature and protect 30% of our planet's total land mass and seas by 2030. This '30 × 30' commitment is not about restoring soil, water, plants and animals because it would be a beautiful thing to do. It is, we've finally realized, a question of our own survival.

However, 2030 is just a heartbeat away and, with barely 2–3% of Earth's land currently ecologically intact, is this goal even remotely realistic? Meeting it will mean going far beyond protecting or improving existing national parks and nature reserves. We're going to have to find a lot more land for nature, including in our own backyards.

Collectively, gardens can make an enormous contribution. The US has 2.3 million km² (888,000 mi²) of residential 'yards' – three times the area of Texas. In England, twenty-three million private gardens occupy an area four times larger than all National Nature Reserves combined. Yet most of these gardens are dominated by monoculture lawns, pesticides and herbicides. They may look green but ecologically they're biological deserts.

Imagine if every garden was managed in a way that sustains life, becoming a miniature ecosystem in its own right. Gardens are close to our hearts, places where we love to be. But by changing our mindset, even just a little, we can create spaces that also welcome other creatures and help conserve – and even restore – precious resources. Consider it 'pocket rewilding', a place where the gardener becomes the keystone species, a trigger for a cascade of rich and wonderful life.

Much of this change in mindset is about challenging our own aesthetics. It's about shedding the preconceived ideas we've grown up with, and questioning our obsession with doing things a particular way. It is, in essence, about rewilding ourselves. The gardeners in this book are thinking radically differently, creating spaces that are not only beautiful but restorative – for nature and for us. They are life-changing, empowering and collectively sustaining.

Faced with planetary crisis, it's easy to feel impotent and despairing. What difference can an individual make in the face of such vast and seemingly insurmountable problems? The answer, as gardeners around the globe are discovering, is to create a little patch of hope in your own backyard. Together, we *can* change the world. Will you join us?

Isabella Tree

Introduction

'Another world is not only possible, she's on her way. Maybe many of us won't be here to greet her, but on a quiet day, if I listen very carefully, I can hear her breathing.'

– Arundhati Roy, author, activist and essayist

We're in the throes of a green and global revolution. All over the world people are nurturing patches of land and seeking new ways to forge connections with nature. Gone are the days of twee ornamental Edens and immaculate confections – today's gardens and green spaces are at the vanguard of positive change, modern-day crucibles for ideas and innovation. From Toronto to Taipei, green-fingered thinkers and pioneering plant people are harnessing the power of the wild to quietly find small-scale strategies to solve stubborn, complex problems that are leaving governments and local communities around the world flailing. At last, gardens are being championed for what they can do – reverse the biodiversity crisis, save water, prevent drought, transform mental health, bridge social divides, educate vulnerable children, reimagine polluting industries and provide much reason for optimism in a rapidly changing world.

Gardens, like all works of art, are a reflection of our cultural sensibilities and where we are in the world. To look at gardens past is to travel through history, from the Arcadian curves of Capability Brown to the ornate excess of French Baroque. And today is no different. But where we are is alarming: teetering on the brink of climate collapse, environmentally exhausted, socially stretched and worn thin. We need gardens more than ever – for their power to repair, heal and nourish our broken world, to empower us to change the systems that no longer serve us and the planet and to reimagine ways of doing things. Luckily, gardens can do it all.

The magic of gardens is apparent to all who have (or have access to) one, and as a garden designer, I have the enormous good fortune of seeing the benefits of gardens up close every day. I grew up surrounded by bucolic green, a privilege that was entirely lost on me until I found myself living surrounded by grey, in a polluted South Asian city, ducking in and out of air-conditioned buildings for six years with barely a banana palm to my name. A change in career to garden design followed shortly after returning to the UK, a subconscious insurance policy to guarantee a lifetime of communing with nature and helping others do the same. For many, this eureka moment happened during the COVID-19 pandemic – whether you were a have or have not, the deep appreciation or aching need for a green space became undeniable.

If you look at any of the headline issues that regularly hog the front pages, there are very few that gardens and access to green spaces couldn't help. Pollution, species extinction, obesity, food poverty, child poverty, mental health, loneliness, drought, flooding...the list continues. Gardens provide such a cornucopia

Succulents hanging in a greenhouse. →

of benefits, it feels absurd that they don't command more social capital. Bang for buck, input for output, you'd be hard-pressed to find something so deliriously simple that can deliver so much. In fact, the only limiting factor is our access to them (which has declined in telling and chilling parallel alongside our growing ill-health and environmental dysfunction).

Thankfully, in researching this book, I have discovered legions of gardeners and designers all over the world who are tapping the power of green spaces, to ensure everyone (birds and bees included) has access to the benefits found in gardens. In a world of information overload and apocalyptic forecasts, it's hard to overstate how much galvanizing hope and optimism this has delivered. The people I have spoken to, the ideas they have shared and the gardens shown in these pages represent a global tapestry of positive change that is well underway. It has given me much needed faith on days when the vast complexity of it all threatens to overwhelm. My hope is that it will have the same effect on you, and perhaps also stir an urge to reach for the *hori hori* (a Japanese weeding tool) and revisit the idea of a garden anew. Because all of us – gardeners, designers, allotment dwellers or those yet to plunge their hands into the soil – can harness the wildly undervalued power of gardens and become a vital link in this vast, borderless mosaic of change. Together, we might just save the world.

How to use this book

This book is both clarion call and celebration. It proves that solutions to our greatest challenges lie in the simple, ancient act of making gardens. Divided into five chapters, it features gardens of every scale from around the world to illustrate how green spaces can radically transform both people and planet.

The benefits of gardens on our natural world are as vast and varied as the ecosystems themselves. *Chapter One begins with repair.* Gardens have the power to restore lost habitats, reverse acute biodiversity loss and repair land and soil worn thin by industry, agriculture and war. They lock in carbon and unlock corridors for wildlife that have been pushed to the margins. Simultaneously, they can repel heat, drain water and absorb pollution, breathing life back into an ecosystem driven to near-total exhaustion.

But the restorative power of gardens extends beyond nature. They are also places of agency, resilience and justice. *Chapter Two explores how gardens can empower us.* Gardens can be a bridge to aspects of our lives that have been taken from us or have fallen out of reach, reconnecting us to purpose, memory and dignity. Adults in custody serving multiple life sentences, deemed a danger to society, find space to be vulnerable in a garden. Refugees and displaced people living in the liminal world of tented cities reclaim fragments of home through the nurturing of plants. Gardens in schools ignite curiosity and lifelong respect for the natural world among children, hosting lessons that cross boundaries from science to art. Crucially, gardens can challenge social structures: the inequality of access to green space, and the disproportionate impact of climate change on the most vulnerable, makes restoring equilibrium a fight for social justice. They are at their core great teachers – a key to untangling history, a lens on the incorruptible cycle of life and a reminder of our place in the world.

Chapter Three turns to nourishment. In an age of industrial food systems and frayed supply chains, gardens offer a direct, sustainable path to better food and health. Britain alone could grow eight times more fruit and veg if all underused green spaces were cultivated. Around the world, innovations in urban growing – like Paris's rooftop farms or Taipei's motorway permaculture – are reclaiming space and reconnecting people with food. By doing so, they strengthen resilience, improve diets and offer a more sustainable model of living. Alongside feeding our bodies, gardens also nourish us emotionally. They reconnect us with rhythms of life that modernity has eroded, enabling us to find meaning, memory and solace in the act of cultivation.

Chapter Four examines how gardens heal. Faced with modern crises of stress, isolation and declining wellbeing, science is catching up with what we instinctively know: nature is essential. From the calming effects of forest bathing to soil bacteria that boost mental health, our need for wildness is real – and measurable. Green spaces soothe our nervous systems, strengthen communities and help us remember that we are part of nature, not separate from it.

Finally, *Chapter Five embraces reimagination.* Gardens are not only a means of repair, empowerment, nourishment and healing – they are also a source of invention. The ways we make gardens, and the ways gardens make us, can push us to consider other ways of living. This demands courage. To reimagine a place or material takes grit: abandoned quarries, mounds of redundant concrete or inherited systems of thought all require us to work longer, risk more and make mistakes along the way. To reimagine the role of the gardener – and grant it the respect it deserves – is to stand firm against naysayers. Happily, there are people and organizations across the globe who remain undeterred by such challenges. Their ideas are redefining what it means to create and build in the modern world, paving the way for the rest of us to follow.

A final but important ambition for this book is that it be useful – beautiful and full of inspiration, yes, but inspiration that we can replicate ourselves. Each garden is presented through this lens: what has this garden done that we can do too? Alongside, you'll find a glossary of strategies, materials and ideas – from biodynamics to guerrilla gardening – intended as a practical resource and handbook. Finally, a series of profiles is woven into the main body of the book, highlighting the people who are leading the garden revolution by pioneering new research, building grassroots networks and championing ideas that improve both the quality of our green spaces and the quality of our lives, whether urban, rural or even digital.

Despite the amount of ground covered, this book is by no means exhaustive. It represents an edited selection of the people, places and projects I discovered during the course of the research, but I could have filled two volumes, such is the wealth of knowledge, passion and expertise out there. I hope reading it will deliver as much hope and optimism as researching it has given me. The answers are all already here, and millions of people are reaping the rewards of a greener world. All we have to do is join them.

Theme Colour Code

You can read this book in many ways. Throughout the chapters, there are threads that connect the projects and stories together. Use the coloured line next to the project title to find out which of the themes shown here it relates to – each of which is vital for sustaining our world – and then seek out the others elsewhere in the book.

Climate resilience

Biodiversity boost

Mental wellbeing

Emotional resilience

Urban growing

Building community

Contemporary take on tradition

Material use and innovation

Educate and empower

Food security

Tangled moss-covered branches in Wistman's Wood, in England's Dartmoor National Park. →

Cacti and succulents in The Huntingdon Desert Garden, in San Marino, California. →

Green bamboo, or *Phyllostachys bissetii*, grows quickly in the mountainous regions of Asia. →

R

EPAIR

Perhaps the most predictable beneficiary of great gardens is nature herself. Gardens are a vital tool in the fight against the environmental collapse we're edging ever closer towards. They can restore habitats (see Glossary) driven to near extinction, coax wildlife populations back to full health and heal land and soils exhausted by our voracious appetites. They absorb the most toxic by-products of modern excess, filter pollutants from waterways and serve as invaluable carbon sequestration systems. Our planet needs all this and more.

The degradation of the natural world over the last century - particularly in the past fifty years - is hard to overstate. Each year brings record-breaking temperatures, with CO_2 levels now more than double what they were before the Industrial Revolution. Global warming is having a catastrophic effect on weather patterns: more devastating storms, longer droughts, more frequent floods and shorter, warmer winters. The climate emergency has led to a 73% decline in monitored global wildlife populations over the last fifty years, as measured by the Living Planet Index (LPI). It has also devastated human communities - wreaking havoc on human populations forcibly removed from their homes with livelihoods rendered untenable. And of course, the impact is particularly cruel on those in the Global South, who bear the least responsibility yet pay the highest cost.

In the vast, interconnected system of our environment, many of these losses compound one another, creating a multiplier effect. When swathes of rainforest are axed, this doesn't just decimate one of our most reliable CO_2 absorption systems, it disrupts the global water cycle. A reduction in Amazonian rainforest means less rain not only locally, but also thousands of miles away, compounding droughts in places already facing water scarcity. Finding a way to break this destructive cycle - to intervene in these vast global systems - can feel overwhelming, even insurmountable. Amid the raucous din, a few truths remain inarguable: the planet is far too hot, and we must wean ourselves off fossil fuels if we are to stem (though not reverse) the rising temperatures. But how we achieve this is far from clear. We're snarled up in a system so colossal and entrenched that individual efforts can feel impotent and futile. Confronted with the enormity of the crisis, even our most well-intentioned attempts to reduce, reuse and recycle can feel like insignificant rounding errors.

The rhetoric around how we can effect change lurches wildly from exhausted despair to energized pragmatism then swiftly back to frustration and anger, with many of us feeling a mix of all these emotions in any given week. Climate change remains maddeningly polarized, often weaponized to stoke political differences rather than generate consensus. With the proliferation of misinformation so widespread, conversations seem to constantly teeter on the edge of hysteria and hyperbole. For the climate-conscientious among us, cast adrift in this turbulent sea of data and disinformation, identifying actions that feel purposeful - and restore a sense of agency - can be a relentless and often demoralizing task. As Sex Pistols frontman and professional rebel John Lydon once famously said, 'anger is an energy' - but the question is: how to make it a galvanizing one?

One strategy is to refocus at a much more micro level. We may not be able to change big systems overnight, but we can change our immediate environment. And in doing so, we might end up having an impact on those things we thought were beyond our control - an argument Naomi Klein powerfully makes in her book *This Changes Everything: Capitalism vs. the Climate.* Klein talks about how grassroots and community-driven initiatives are not just important, but essential in combating climate change. A web of small, local actions, she suggests, can collectively challenge systemic issues and inspire broader movements. This idea - that interconnected, incremental changes can drive profound impact - is well understood and has been adopted by many environmental organizations and movements. Permaculture (see Glossary), for instance, is built on local, self-sufficient systems that obfuscate reliance on global supply chains, forming a regenerative model in their own right. Bill McKibben, founder of the global climate organization 350.org, is a passionate advocate for this kind of decentralized local activism and energy.

In her much-needed book *What If We Get It Right?*, marine biologist and policy expert Ayana Elizabeth Johnson argues that personalization is the key to effective change. Rather than just ticking the standard boxes (vote, protest, reduce your carbon footprint) she urges us to think more about what we as individuals can uniquely offer. What are you good at? What is the work that needs doing? And what brings you joy? For me, that answer is gardens and I hope the fact that you're reading this book means the same is true for you. Gardens are a powerful tool

← **Landscape designer Ximena Nazal's garden in Valparaiso, Chile, is a sanctuary for the country's endangered plants (pp.48-51).**

in fighting the effects of a changing climate. They serve as micro-environments for ecological restoration, helping repair and sustain the natural world while fostering a deeper connection between humans and nature.

The variety of site-specific responses to the challenges posed by climate change are a powerful homage to the planet's glorious biodiversity (see Glossary) and a reassuring sign that the tide is turning against the scourge of grey homogenization. In New York, native planting schemes in public parks are attracting populations of monarch butterflies and herons. In Singapore, vibrant and biodiverse ecosystems coexist alongside ultramodern urban life. And in the UK, rewilding has been adapted to a more domestic scale, proving that plot size need not be a hindrance to designing ecologically rich and complex habitats that support a kaleidoscope of insects and pollinators.

Gardens are also proving to be vital components in the (less glamorous but no less essential) water management machine. In Sheffield, Sustainable Drainage Systems (SuDS – see Glossary) planting has been reimagined into technicolour splendour by the likes of Nigel Dunnett and Zac Tudor, helping to mitigate urban flooding. In Singapore, large-scale rain gardens, such as those at Jurong Lake Gardens, work hard to filter pollutants and plastics from tropical runoff. Elsewhere, plants play an important role in phytoremediation – the removal of contaminants and heavy metals from soil, water and air using plants. In Milan, the Bosco Verticale demonstrates how covering skyscrapers in species particularly suited to this task can significantly improve air quality and oxygen levels in dense urban areas.

At the other end of the scale, plants adapted to extreme heat are helping to make cities more liveable – and more beautiful – by providing shade and reducing the urban heat island (UHI) effect. In high-risk regions, they can also play a critical role in fire mitigation. In Australia, a country increasingly vulnerable to wildfires, planting broad-leaved, fire-resistant plants or dense carpets of water-retentive succulents can help halt the crackle of the wildfire in its tracks.

And while some of these gardens are vast, the majority are not. John Little's garden in Essex, for example, is a masterclass in creating microhabitats – often built from materials more widely regarded as waste. These gardens are the theory of interconnectedness in action – millions of small, diverse patches of green attached to suburban houses from Manila to Miami, which together form an ecological force far greater than the sum of their parts. They are proof that meaningful change is within our reach. Many of these gardens require very little in the way of infrastructure or investment. They're low (but not no) intervention, and very high reward.

Perhaps the greatest restoration project we have on our hands is mending our relationship with nature. How can we understand what is happening in the natural world if we don't know it intimately? According to David Godshall (interviewed on page 218), one of the key purposes of gardens is to make humans more resilient stewards of the land. By tending our own patches of green in a more thoughtful and considered way, not only are we repairing ecosystems and services, but we're also repairing our broken connection to the natural world – a task that is as vital as repairing the land itself.

The waterfall at the Chelsea Australian Garden →
in Olinda, Australia, relies on rainwater runoff
(pp.62–5).

Harvest rainwater to sustain you through the dry season

The Ruins
Valle de Bravo, Mexico
Estudio Ome

Harvesting, storing and reusing rainwater is a challenge faced by gardeners all over the world. Doing it in a way that is both practical and beautiful, and doesn't require vast underground water tanks, takes skill and imagination.

This project is part of a pioneering sustainable housing community masterminded by Mexican developer Alberto Kritzler. Part nature reserve, part commune, it's a model whereby people and planet are working together for mutual benefit. Prior to development, the land had been exhausted by decades of deforestation and agriculture. Today, eighty families live on the 450-acre estate, demonstrating how regenerative design strategies can preserve and replenish the land.

The garden, designed by Estudio Ome, prioritizes a closed-loop rainwater-harvesting system. To make the most of the region's extreme rainfall in the wet season, a lake was created to collect and store the water, functioning as a cistern for the house. Recognizing that lakes can lose their aesthetic appeal as they dry, Estudio Ome designed a series of concentric rings within the lake that are revealed as the water recedes. Each ring features a wet garden planted at every level, the deepest of which doubles as a natural swimming pool. Like a slowly turning clock, the garden becomes a living measure of time. A palette of predominantly native plants and local stone helps the newly built house sit gently within the landscape. The result is a garden that is both deeply practical and poetic.

Build waterways to attract wildlife and reduce flood risk

Jurong Lake Gardens
Jurong East, Singapore
Henning Larsen

Until recently, this vibrant green lung was a decimated post-industrial landscape, stripped bare during Singapore's rapid development in the 1960s. As part of a nationwide commitment to rejuvenating natural assets, a five-year project saw the urban park restored to its former incarnation as a species-rich multi-habitat park comprising swamp forest, wetlands and grasslands as well as extensive play and recreation areas for residents.
In doing so, the wildlife has returned in spades. Native and migratory bird species including paddyfield pipit, long-tailed shrike, brown shrike, savanna nightjar, common kestrel, black-winged kite and intermediate egret all flock here to find food and shelter in the grasslands.

But the gardens also act as an important tool in Singapore's defence against climate change. As a tropical coastal island, Singapore is particularly vulnerable to sea-level rises, extreme rainfall and flooding. Where once there was a single straight drain taking unprocessed stormwater from the city to the lake, there is now nearly a kilometre (half a mile) of braided waterways wending their way through the gardens. These naturalized streams slow stormwater, channelling runoff through the gardens so it arrives clean at Jurong Lake – an entirely natural, low-impact method of processing stormwater that helps mitigate against the risks posed by increased flooding while seamlessly integrating a complex habitat into Singapore's evolving landscape.

Watch closely and take notes to boost wildlife

Brooklyn Bridge Park
New York City, USA
Michael Van Valkenburgh Associates Inc

According to the World Wildlife Fund's (WWF) *Living Planet Report 2022*, wildlife populations have declined by an average of 69% in the past fifty years. Much of this is due to disruption and loss of natural habitats to make way for human progress, agriculture and industry. One of the most pressing challenges of our time is how to integrate wildlife habitats into human spaces. Thankfully, the solution is relatively simple: planning and managing landscapes with the primary goal of boosting biodiversity. The key to this is careful observation, conscientious data collection and a willingness to adjust plans while keeping this simple goal in mind. Brooklyn Bridge Park is a best-in-class example of this methodology in action, demonstrating how gentle and thoughtful management can dramatically boost wildlife populations even if that green space was, until recently, a defunct cargo and shipping complex on the edge of New York City. Spanning two kilometres (1.2 miles) over Brooklyn's waterfront, the park connects the city to the shoreline and provides vital storm buffers in the face of climate change. But it's the management strategy that delivers such astonishing ecological value. The vast planting scheme spans a variety of ecologies and microclimates – a patchwork of ecosystems – each tended by a small, devolved team of dedicated horticulturists referred to as 'curators'. Each curator is responsible for 0.7 to 1.2 acres of land – a high land-to-labour ratio for a public park.

The curators' role is to observe their patch, look and listen carefully to what is happening – how is a plant performing both individually and as part of the broader ecology? What wildlife is making use of this plant? For example, noting that song sparrows are overwintering in the rose mallows would mean shifting the cutting-back programme to allow for this. Observing that the bog beans in the wetlands have become a popular spot for herons and bull frogs would mean encouraging more bog beans. This strategy of continuous and careful observation with the goal of increasing biodiversity has seen a rich variety of wildlife make its home there. The teams actively track wildlife species and keep detailed and downloadable records on their website of host plants, nesting habits and migratory patterns of native birds, bees and other insects that we could all be providing with vital sources of food and shelter. It's a simple and remarkably effective strategy, but one that involves care, attention and time, resources that are often sorely lacking in both civic garden maintenance, and in society more broadly.

Create green lungs in the sky to breathe more easily

Bosco Verticale
Milan, Italy
Stefano Boeri

Air pollution is the single biggest environmental health risk in the world and is linked to millions of deaths every year. Trees and plants are among our most powerful allies in the fight against it, but in high-density cities, planting at the scale needed to meaningfully shift air quality is a serious challenge. However, Bosco Verticale has set a new standard for metropolitan reforestation, proving that a lack of access to land is no obstacle to enjoying the pollution-busting benefits of a forest.

The two high-rise residential towers in Milan's business district have been planted with over 10,000 plants, 800 of which are trees. This has created vertical forests that suck an astonishing 20,000 kg (44,000 lbs) of carbon out of the atmosphere annually. They also filter out fine dust particles, protect against heat and noise pollution from traffic below, and create a radically different relationship between architecture and nature. The project is the brainchild of architect Stefano Boeri, inspired by a novel about a boy who abandons *terra firma* to spend the rest of his life inhabiting a kingdom in the trees. Bringing this to life was fiendishly complex. Years of research went into selecting species resilient enough to thrive in the exposed conditions of a high-rise and deliver maximum air-purifying impact. Engineers devised systems to anchor trees securely against high winds, while the logistics of irrigation and maintenance were solved with an innovative solution: a team of aerial arborists, akin to the professionals who clean skyscraper windows, now tend to the forest in the sky.

Having overcome these challenges, Bosco Verticale has been hailed as a milestone in urban reforestation, sparking a wave of similar projects now in development in cities including Taipei, Bogotá and Toronto.

Sue Stuart-Smith Psychiatrist, Psychotherapist and Author

For Sue Stuart-Smith – psychiatrist, psychotherapist and author of the best-selling book *The Well Gardened Mind* – our personal health and the health of the planet are inextricably linked. This is because we are nature, and always have been. For thousands of years, humans evolved in lockstep with the natural world, a mutual relationship that shaped us both. Our recent alienation from nature is a mere blip in an otherwise long, symbiotic relationship since the dawn of time. This is why gardening is so important: it reconnects us to our roots, both literal and metaphorical. But in today's world, many of us are not reaping the rewards of gardening. Quite the opposite – we often feel excluded from it. For many, gardens can seem intimidating: soil is even referred to as 'dirt' in America and treated accordingly. We treat the Earth with a level of disregard that we would never extend to other people or even to animals, by dousing it in chemicals and toxins without thought. To move forward, we must find our way back to a relationship with nature. Gardens, Sue suggests, can help us to do that.

Sue discovered the power of gardens after marrying renowned garden designer Tom Stuart-Smith. It was vegetables that got her hooked. The simple pleasure of growing something that she could cook and eat at her kitchen table proved hard to resist. There was something deeply empowering about knowing her food was healthy, local and grown just steps away from the kitchen door. As she fell in love with gardening (and a gardener), the garden soon became an integral part of her life – a place of joy, reflection and connection with nature. As a psychotherapist, Sue began to notice striking parallels between gardening and personal growth. In 2015, she set out to explore these connections more deeply, embarking on years of research that culminated in *The Well Gardened Mind*. Drawing on a wealth of epidemiological evidence, the book revealed just how profoundly green spaces can support mental health and help alleviate a wide range of conditions. At the time, this idea was still viewed as somewhat 'fringe'. The fact that gardens are now recognized as a powerful tool for positive mental health is in no small part thanks to Sue's book.

Part of what makes gardens such powerful therapeutic tools is their ability to restore hope. With eco-anxiety on the rise – especially among young people – many feel completely paralysed by apocalyptic climate predictions, leading to apathy and anxiety. But gardens, Sue says, offer an antidote: 'They're something we can all do, and we can actually make a significant difference with them.' In the face of overwhelming global challenges, they offer a tangible way to take action. They combat the sense of powerlessness and are potent symbols of nature's ability to heal. By planting with wildlife in mind, we can make genuine gains in reversing biodiversity. By growing our own vegetables, we support our physical health, reduce food costs and gain a sense of self-reliance. Sue recalls a moment at Rikers Island, New York's largest jail, where one man's eyes lit up upon discovering vegetables he'd planted beginning to grow: 'It's like printing money!' Seeing this change is hugely powerful as it restores our faith in recovery and our sense of agency. But, crucially, it also restores our relationship with the natural world: 'What's good for the planet is what's good for us,' Sue asserts. 'When did we lose that?'

Unlocking the benefits of gardens depends on access, yet, as Sue points out, 'many children have no access to nature,' and nature deprivation in cities is a major issue. The impact is twofold: not only are people shut out of the wellbeing gardens can provide, but our disconnection from nature deepens.

While researching her book, Sue visited Windy City Harvest's Youth Farm in Chicago, a community garden offering green space to at-risk children. 'Getting their hands in the dirt was absolutely transformative,' she says. Witnessing this in action was transformative for Sue too: 'it really sowed a seed for me.' It inspired the Serge Hill Project for Gardening, Creativity and Health in Hertfordshire (see page 182), which she now runs to provide garden access to those who lack it. She likens gardening to a conversation – 'nature does her bit, and then we respond, and so it goes on, like a conversation'. The Serge Hill Project, she hopes, is the beginning of that exchange.

There are signs of progress, with gardens increasingly used in social prescribing to support mental health – something Sue hopes to expand at the Serge Hill Project. But this depends on receptive GPs and accessible garden spaces. Currently, Thrive is the only charity in the UK offering training in Social and Therapeutic Horticulture, and access to services remains a postcode lottery. Policy is siloed, with gardens still overlooked as part of public health.

Despite these systemic challenges, Sue is hopeful and pragmatic: 'we don't need more evidence, it's all there – so we're just getting on with it' – continuing the conversation we began with nature many years ago.

Harness the benefits of rewilding on a domestic scale

Knepp Walled Garden
Shipley, West Sussex, UK
Tom Stuart-Smith and James Hitchmough

Despite being the subject of considerable (and I would argue largely unfounded) controversy, rewilding is, at its heart, simply about restoring natural ecological processes. The goal is habitat restoration and, as a consequence, a reversal of biodiversity loss and much more besides. There are plenty of well-researched studies that demonstrate these benefits in action, however, they are largely reliant on huge swathes of land – farms and nature reserves that have committed thousands of acres to rewilding. But for the millions of us working with considerably smaller plots of land, how do we apply the principles of rewilding in a more domestic setting? And does it work on a more diminutive scale? The Knepp Castle Estate is one such example. Twenty years ago, Charlie Burrell and Isabella Tree – themselves and their land exhausted by farming – opted to try something new. They decided to rewild their hitherto intensively farmed land and wait and see what happened. The results have been astounding. Knepp now boasts breeding nightingales and turtle doves, as well as dormice, and it is lauded as proof of nature's ability to recover when given half a chance.

It's no surprise then that they have chosen the estate's walled garden as an experimental test bed for rewilding on a smaller scale. Once a croquet lawn and series of immaculately tended ornamental beds, the garden has been redesigned with ecological complexity in mind. This is to create a complex mosaic of habitats (as you would over a large swathe of rewilded land) but on a much smaller scale. This has been achieved through simple interventions such as creating three-dimensional humps and hollows of varying soil conditions, which support a greater diversity of plant species, and therefore insect and wildlife species too. Over 900 species of plants have been introduced, and the garden, still in its infancy, has already seen a 33.3% uplift in the number of invertebrate species recorded since baseline surveys.

Leading the team is head gardener Charlie Harpur. 'Complexity is key, in both the design and the management of a garden,' he tells me. When designing a garden, he encourages thinking about it as a kaleidoscope of different habitats and how you can diversify those habitat types within your garden, for example, shaded wooded areas versus free-draining and more exposed areas. And if your garden is small, think about it in relation to your neighbours. 'Whatever is missing could be an area to focus on in your garden,' he says. When we see our gardens not as islands but as part of a bigger living mosaic, however small the plot, we're contributing to a richer and wilder world.

Reimagine industrial sites with resilient naturalistic planting communities

The High Line
New York City, USA
Piet Oudolf (Planting)

The High Line has become a poster-girl of urban regeneration – a blueprint for what can be achieved in forgotten post-industrial landscapes. Built on an abandoned railway line stretching from the Meatpacking District to Hudson Rail Yards in Manhattan, it is an icon in New York's already heavyweight cultural portfolio and the living embodiment of preservation as a strategy for sustainability. A public space once slated for demolition by Mayor Rudy Giuliani has been reborn as a textured, pathless landscape that sequesters over 1.3 tonnes of atmospheric carbon annually, thanks to more than 750 newly planted trees and tens of thousands of perennials in a scheme designed by famed Dutch landscape designer Piet Oudolf.

Inspired by the site's original self-seeded landscape, the planting is perhaps the most emblematic of Oudolf's signature style – a celebration of perennials and grasses across all four seasons of interest, chosen for their seedheads, movement and structural beauty as well as their flowers. Plants are combined to mimic the communities they would appear in naturally, creating not just a distinctly naturalistic aesthetic, but also ecologically resilient schemes. These richly layered plantings have doubled the number of species across the site, which in turn is attracting new populations of pollinators and beneficial insects – not to mention seven million human visitors a year and a revitalized economy for the surrounding districts – right in the heart of the world's most iconic metropolis.

Use planted steps and terraces to boost biodiversity

Kampung Admiralty
Woodlands, Singapore
Henning Larsen/WOHA Architects

Persuading stakeholders to carve out space for planting in dense urban developments, where land is at a premium, is tough. It can be harder still for designers to create real ecological benefits on the slithers of space available. What generates value is a rich and diverse mix of plants carefully selected for the site, which will encourage complex ecological interactions. Despite the scarcity of land, Singapore has emerged as a global leader in urban greening, thanks to its steadfast Green City policy that places landscaping and biodiversity at the centre of its urban-development strategy. It also helps that the tropical South Asian climate fosters optimal conditions for plant growth and abundance. Nevertheless, the Kampung Admiralty, a mixed-use building that includes a residential complex for the elderly, is an innovative example of how small areas of space can be utilized to create a rich and complex ecosystem.

Set across a series of rooftop terraces, the building's green areas exceed its footprint, in a planting scheme that uses the terraces of the building to create a hill-like planting arrangement, with a total of 730 trees and 80,000 shrubs. The layered design of the building allows for different planting levels, mimicking those found in natural ecosystems, creating a truly functional habitat. The result is an immersive, dynamic, community rooftop park that looks and feels like it's brimming with life – because it is.

Learn about plant communities for a garden that really thrives

Hermannshof
Baden-Württemberg, Germany
Cassian Schmidt

All too often, planting in public gardens and parks is dominated by evergreen shrubs and trees. These may tick the 'year-round interest' box (though only just), but they provide almost zero seasonal interest and little ecological benefit either. These schemes are reliant on a narrow palette of plants that are unable to offer much in the way of diversity or visual interest, but are repeatedly planted across acres of precious public land because they're perceived to be 'low maintenance'. In reality, the upkeep of these static displays of plants involves armies of hedge trimmers and leaf blowers, as well as lots of high-intensity bedding plants to give the requisite hit of colour come spring and summer.

Hermannshof, a public park in Germany, has long been recognized for its ambitious and exuberant planting schemes across multiple habitats and zones. However, this style of planting is not feasible for every public landscape. Determined to offer an alternative to uninspired planting, former director Cassian Schmidt developed a planting system based on the principles of plant sociology – the study of how plant communities function together – but that also delivered high aesthetic value.

By designing plant mixes that mimic naturally occurring communities, the Hermannshof team created schemes that are both ecologically functional and visually compelling. Plants are grouped by height, texture or colour, with species selection tailored to site conditions and calculated on a per-square-metre basis. Once planted in a seemingly random but ecologically considered matrix, these combinations form vibrant, resilient plant communities that thrive with minimal intervention.

The success of this approach has spurred collaboration with universities to trial plant mixes for different climates and soil conditions. These test plots are being monitored over five years to assess long-term performance and refine the methodology – paving the way for a new standard in sustainable, biodiverse public planting.

Create a sanctuary to protect species under threat

Vivero San Gabriel
Valparaiso, Chile
Ximena Nazal

Chile is one of the most biodiverse countries on the planet, 4,000 kilometres (2,400 miles) in length, with habitats from the high Andean mountains to the Atacama Desert and deep, lush valleys and forests. However, climate change is making much of this rich landscape increasingly uninhabitable, with temperatures regularly soaring above 40 °C (100 °F) in once-temperate regions. This has caused mass human migration to cooler regions, and has in turn displaced much of the country's endemic flora.

Ximena Nazal is a landscape designer and gardener who has spent a lifetime studying and collecting plants from her beloved country, and learning from the natural world to create beautiful and resilient gardens. Never has this been more prescient. Her garden, which is the fruit of thirty years of tinkering and experimentation, is both extraordinarily beautiful and an increasingly important sanctuary for Chile's threatened flora. Over 30% of the species in the garden are native to Chile and many are critically endangered. It has become a large-scale experiment in xeriscaping – a way of gardening that eliminates the need for irrigation. At Vivero San Gabriel, plants from arid climates all over the world – the Mediterranean, South Africa and Chilean deserts – thrive, mostly with little to no water input. Sculptural and otherworldly agaves sit proudly among shimmering native grasses and Mediterranean alliums make up the 'wild genetic pool', in a sanctuary of rare botanical curiosities collected and protected by Ximena for future generations to enjoy.

Divert rainwater to create urban rain gardens

Grey to Green
Sheffield, UK
Zac Tudor/Sheffield City Council

Historically, rainfall in cities has been designed to flow quickly through a network of pipes and gullies into the mains drainage system. However, with increasingly extreme weather patterns and rainfall containing a host of contaminants, from pollutants to heavy metals, our water systems are overwhelmed. This results in ever more severe flooding in towns and cities. Where once natural water catchment areas existed, today non-permeable hard landscaping simply diverts water into an already strained system. The solution? Strategic planting through Sustainable Drainage Systems (SuDS), which can transform cityscapes by reducing rainwater runoff and creating ecologically diverse planting schemes with dramatic visual impact. Sheffield's Grey to Green project is a best-in-class example of a retrofit SuDS scheme and is preventing 24,000 bathtubs of water from entering Sheffield's sewage treatment works each year. Large planting schemes have been reintegrated into areas of the city that were a sea of concrete not so long ago. Instead, rich and ecologically varied planting beds that can tolerate both heavy rainfall and a summer of very little have brought colour and life back to Sheffield's city centre. They are also performing a vital water management task too. The camber of the roads and footpaths directs excess water directly into the planting beds, where it safely and slowly passes through them, taking pressure off the drains and irrigating the planting on the way. While this may seem like a simple, even obvious solution to a problem, it took the dedication and vision of Sheffield landscape architect Zac Tudor to convince stakeholders that a plant-filled urban landscape could deliver this much benefit, but deliver it did. The project's success has led to its expansion; today, Grey to Green stands as a landmark project that has turned SuDS into one of the city's attractions – something truly remarkable.

Plant trees to create a microclimate in a desert

Al Fay Park
Abu Dhabi, United Arab Emirates
SLA

In the subtropical and arid climes of Abu Dhabi, temperatures can regularly hit 40 °C (100 °F) making lazing about outdoors in parks unfeasible for much of the day, and much of the year. However, using trees and planting as part of a microclimate optimization strategy can transform a once inhospitable desert into a lush oasis, opening up whole new parks for people to enjoy. At Al Fay Park, designed by SLA, trees have been chosen for their ability to provide shade and reduce solar radiation, and planted at a density that guarantees a cool and comfortable microclimate under the glare of the desert sun. The plant palette was researched in a year-long study by SLA's biologists to ensure a scheme that would not only tolerate the conditions but thrive and evolve into a healthy self-sustaining ecosystem.

The result is a scheme that is predominantly native and well adapted to the harsh environment, using species like the ghaf tree (*Prosopis cineraria*), which were grown in local desert nurseries. Winding paths offer immersive forest experiences in the most unlikely of climates, and a modern irrigation system using recirculated water means that it uses 40% less water than traditional parks. Other design interventions include sloping entrances, which funnel a cool southern breeze through the park, making it a city hub for sports and socializing, even on sweltering days. With Al Fay Park, SLA has set a new standard for how to create nature-rich environments in the megacities of the Middle East and proven that, even in the desert, you can still create the coolest place in town.

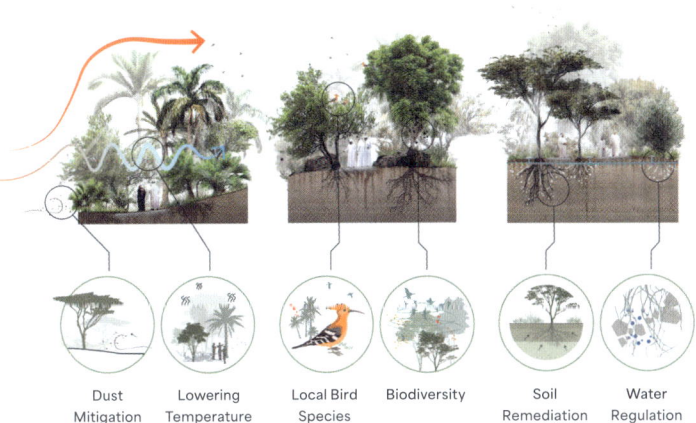

| Dust Mitigation | Lowering Temperature | Local Bird Species | Biodiversity | Soil Remediation | Water Regulation |

Collect rainwater to create an alternative soundscape

Tomsgårdsvej
Copenhagen, Denmark
SLA

In a changing climate, what many countries are dealing with is not extreme heat or drought, as the misnomer 'global warming' might suggest, but extreme wet weather – flash flooding, long wet winters and saturated soils that place immense pressure on outdated urban systems. The loss of green spaces in cities has only made matters worse, removing natural systems that once helped absorb and dissipate excess rainwater. But managing extreme rainfall doesn't just bring ecological benefit, it can also open up new sensory opportunities (see Glossary), creating an alternative soundscape to traffic in urban environments.

On Tomsgårdsvej, a main arterial road in northwest Copenhagen with traffic volumes to match, SLA has created a system whereby rainwater runoff from the road is collected and fed into a trickling and burbling water feature, creating a new natural soundscape for residents otherwise plagued by traffic noise. At the heart of the project is an eighty-metre-long (262-ft) sinuous 'water staircase' built from rammed earth (see Glossary). This sculptural feature acts as both a visual centrepiece and a tactile and engaging sensory play space for children. Surrounding it, densely planted quaking aspens (*Populus tremula*), which rustle in the breeze, add further auditory interest.

The result is a courtyard where the experience of sound has been transformed. While the volume of traffic remains unchanged, the presence of water and trees has shifted the sensory balance, providing relief, richness and a greater sense of wellbeing. It's a powerful example of how thoughtful water management can benefit both people and wildlife, turning a functional intervention into a multisensory experience.

Fernanda Rionda Naturalistic Landscape Designer

Like many landscape designers, Fernanda Rionda's journey into the world of landscape architecture was non-linear and serendipitous. Originally trained in International Relations, her path took a transformative turn when the Master's course in History she wanted to enrol on was full. That afternoon, she saw an advert for a diploma in garden design and on discovering the first module focused on the history of gardens, signed up 'and day one of the class, I knew this was what I was going to do for the rest of my life'. The diploma laid the foundations for a career that would come to weave together her background in diplomacy, design, and a profound love for the power that gardens and green spaces have to build identity and meaning.

Today, after two decades of experience and more than 300 projects at every scale, Fernanda stands at the forefront of her profession as the President of the Mexican Society of Landscape Architects (SAPmx). In this role, Fernanda's interests have come full circle; her early education in politics and society and her love of nature work happily in tandem in her capacity as a champion of sustainable and meaningful landscapes across Mexico and Latin America. Under her presidency, she has overseen ambitious initiatives, such as the success of the VI Latin American Landscape Architecture Biennial which was held for the first time outside of Mexico in Medellín, Colombia, in 2024. In doing so, Fernanda's natural affinity with multi-cultural and -lingual collaboration (she was educated in the UK) has facilitated a new era of regional co-operation, elevating the visibility of landscape architects in Latin America and promoting the field as a critical force for improving quality of life and protecting the environment. Today her role is both mentor and advocate, helping to foster a growing community of landscape architects who recognize the essential relationship between nature and the built environment.

Much of this stems from Fernanda's deep love and understanding of naturalistic planting, a movement that had swept through European landscape design, but would only later gain traction in Mexico. When many in Mexico were still mimicking traditional 'European-style' planting schemes, Fernanda was tuning in to the nature-based solutions to be found in naturalistic planting design. Alongside the environmental benefits of a more ecologically minded approach, there were cultural drivers too. In a world awash with globalization and the inevitable homogenization that follows, Fernanda believes that landscape architecture has a unique ability to restore and preserve the distinctiveness of a place – 'landscape does not lie'. While architecture can be repeated anonymously in almost any environment, landscapes are inherently site-specific, shaped by the natural and cultural context in which they exist. Thus it follows that landscapes are not just aesthetic or recreational spaces; they are vital expressions of local identity, capable of healing fractured communities and strengthening social bonds in ways that few other forms of design can.

Through this prism, landscape design is a powerful tool not just in the fight against environmental degradation, but cultural and societal erosion too. 'Landscape architecture has the power to create communities and strengthen social bonds, even having the potential to mend broken ties that have been fractured by violence, migration, and other social phenomena that have persisted for centuries on our planet.'

For Fernanda, the challenge now is reimagining the landscape as an ecological continuum – one that transcends human-imposed boundaries. We need to think big, beyond political borders and holistically to create resilient projects that genuinely integrate *with* their environments and *across* the environment as a whole. There are big rewards if we can do this – mitigating against biodiversity loss, reducing urban heat islands, and navigating water management challenges – all issues that are intensifying across Latin America.

To help facilitate this joined-up thinking, Fernanda is currently involved in a project to develop a species catalogue for a municipality adjacent to Mexico City. The goal is to standardize the use of native and non-invasive exotic species, fostering resilient plant communities that can adapt and thrive within one of the largest metropolitan areas in the world. It's a project that has huge potential to enhance local ecosystems and serves as a model for sustainable urban developments across the region in the future.

Next on her horizon are Mexico's post-industrial landscapes, currently barren and full of untapped potential. Having recently completed a project with Ferromex, Mexico's largest freight train company, where she created a linear park in Mexico City from a disused railway (see page 240), she now has her sights on more. For her, these neglected spaces represent enormous potential – places where environmental regeneration can go hand in hand with community building, social renewal and place-making.

Despite the overwhelming challenges we face, her work gives Fernanda much reason for optimism. Hope lies in the transformative potential of landscape architecture. It's a beacon and a powerful tool for creating sustainable cities and restoring the balance between people and nature, and Fernanda's work is testament to this. In every project, from intimate city courtyards to ambitious regional collaborations, there's a clear message: landscapes are living identities, and through them we can build a better, more connected and more resilient future.

Ward off fire with a rainfall-fed billabong

Chelsea Australian Garden at Olinda
Victoria, Australia
Phillip Johnson Landscapes

While much of the world is wrestling with how to manage excess rainfall and flooding, in Australia the risk of bushfires is becoming ever greater as average temperatures soar and dry seasons extend. For Phillip Johnson and his landscaping practice, improving fire resilience alongside effective water management is central to their work. The Chelsea Australian Garden at Olinda – originally conceived for the RHS Chelsea Flower Show in 2013, where it won 'Best in Show' – is a striking example of this. Entirely off-grid, the garden relies on no mains water or power. Instead, over a million litres of rainwater runoff are captured and redirected to feed a cascading waterfall and naturalistic billabong. This is water that would otherwise contribute to erosion further downstream.

Sensors installed throughout the garden trigger an inbuilt sprinkler system to douse the garden should the threat of fire become too great. So much water is in reserve that it is also used by the local fire brigade. Beyond its role in fire protection, the billabong serves as a rich habitat, attracting kookaburras, wallabies, kangaroos and many species of frog. The combination of water and a rich, diverse palette of native plants – many of which are naturally fire-resistant – creates a garden that is dense, layered, authentically of its place and highly resilient to the vicissitudes of the Australian climate.

Prioritize habitat creation to establish a garden nature reserve

Great Dixter House and Gardens
Northiam, East Sussex, UK
Christopher Lloyd/Fergus Garrett

Great Dixter is one of the UK's most treasured gardens, famed for its exuberant planting, horticultural innovation and its vital role in the industry as an incubator of ideas and talent. Much of this can be credited to Head Gardener, Fergus Garrett, whose boundless passion for both plants and people has shaped Dixter's continued evolution. What is perhaps less well-known is that Great Dixter is also a biodiversity hotspot, supporting an astonishing array of wildlife because of, not in spite of, its ravishing ornamental splendour. Christopher Lloyd, the original owner and creator of the garden at Dixter, was an observant and knowledgeable naturalist, deeply attuned to the complex web of species that populate the land. Continuing this legacy, in the twenty years since he inherited the stewardship of Great Dixter, Garrett has slowly but surely pursued strategies that foster more wildlife and phased out those that don't. Chemical use has been reduced to zero, grass and verges are allowed to grow long, habitat piles (often very beautiful ones) and dead wood are left to create homes for insects and bees, meadows have been expanded, and hedges are allowed to billow and embrace the adjoining land. This all happened organically, following a gut instinct for what would encourage wildlife – and anecdotally it did. The gardens felt alive and humming with activity. But to truly understand the impact, they needed data. In 2017, supported by a Heritage Lottery Fund grant and private donors, a full biodiversity audit was conducted. Surveys and habitat assessments looked at everything from grassland, hedgerows, lichens and mosses, to fungi, fruit trees, birds, mammals, spiders, butterflies and insects. The results were astonishing, revealing a richness of biodiversity usually reserved for Sites of Special Scientific Interest (SSSI). The garden was found to host rare bees, wasps, butterflies and moths, including the very rare white-bellied mining bee (*Andrena gravida*) and the elusive purple emperor butterfly (*Apatura iris*). It also supports an exceptional selection of breeding birds, including the nightingale.

Great Dixter is a reassuring and inspiring masterclass in how ornamental gardens can support conservation, creating a 'garden nature reserve' – and a model for garden biodiversity.

Plant pioneer plants to win hearts and minds

Beech Gardens
The Barbican Estate, London, UK
Nigel Dunnett

The Barbican Estate is the jewel in London's Brutalist crown, built in the 1960s for affluent city professionals and their families as part of a post-war regeneration project. Originally set out in the 1970s, Beech Gardens is effectively a roof garden comprising a large courtyard in the centre of a series of tower blocks, raised above a busy London road. By 2015, the gardens were leaking into the spaces below, and the original design – heavy on bedding plants with a high-maintenance lawn – felt outdated. This presented a rare opportunity to reimagine a scheme more suited to a changing climate.

Navigating the redesign of such an iconic site – one that, aside from the leaks, many residents felt didn't need changing – called for a sensitive and considered approach. A large-scale public consultation with Barbican residents and other site users followed. Concerns included the potential loss of colourful bedding plants, a perceived lack of tree cover and the need for year-round interest. Nigel Dunnett and his team were attentive to these concerns. This was a human landscape, and resident engagement was critical to the scheme's success.

Equally important was the need for the planting to look good from the start. In a high-traffic public space, Nigel recognized that early visual impact was essential to win hearts and minds. To do this, he planted ruderal species – ecological pioneers that are first to colonize disturbed land and pave the way for other species to thrive. They're often quick-flowering, self-seeders with relatively short life-spans. Here, Nigel used white-flowered rose campion (*Lychnis coronaria* 'Alba'), purple top (*Verbena bonariensis*) and garden scabious (*Scabiosa caucasica*) to deliver the initial dopamine hit that encouraged early community engagement in year one, allowing the slower-growing perennials time to mature.

To address concerns about winter interest, Nigel incorporated grasses such as shining moor-grass (*Sesleria nitida*) and swathes of evergreens including spurge (*Euphorbia characias* 'Humpty Dumpty') to deliver a reassuring measure of green through the long, grey winter months. The result is a scheme that deftly navigates the challenging twin briefs of delivering bounty and beauty for people and planet, in the Brutalist heart of London.

EMP

OWER

Beyond fostering physiological and psychological wellbeing, gardens serve as portals to worlds we have been temporarily or permanently separated from, offering a path to healing. A single plant can transport us back to childhood or serve as a vital link to a life lost through war, imprisonment or addiction. Working in gardens can be just as restorative. The simple act of nurturing life from a seed in stark, dehumanizing environments restores much-needed hope and dignity. Plunging our hands into the soil, feeling the dirt under our fingernails and reconnecting with what poet Mary Oliver called 'the nature of things' is a deeply empowering ritual and one that humans have turned to for solace and renewal since time immemorial.

However, for all their wholesome benefit, some gardens conceal a dark underbelly. Botanical gardens house collections of plants from around the world, often stolen by plant hunters as trophies of the British Empire. These gardens were not merely scientific institutions but also repositories of imperial wealth, where plants taken from colonized lands were displayed as symbols of conquest and control. Exotic species were extracted from their native ecosystems, often with little regard for Indigenous Knowledge Systems (IKS) that had nurtured them for generations. Transplanted to Europe, these specimens reinforced narratives of Western superiority and dominion over the so-called 'unknown' or 'wild'. The taxonomy of plants was designed to serve the colonial project – a universal nomenclature that enabled the spoils of conquest to be easily identified and mapped for the oppressors. Plants were often named after the hunters who 'discovered' them and other colonial figures, erasing their local and Indigenous names in the process. In *Botany of Empire*, Banu Subramaniam argues that even European sexual norms were imposed onto plants. Their reproductive systems were interpreted through a rigid, binary, heterosexual lens irrespective of the breathtaking diversity of plant reproductive systems.

We also have empire to thank for the pernicious language used to classify plants as native, non-native, invasive or weeds (see Glossary). Forgotten in these classifications is the fact that European colonialism was responsible for what Subramaniam calls the 'great reshuffling of global biota'. In our relentless pursuit of the exotic, it wasn't just tea, coffee and cocoa that arrived on our shores in Wardian cases, but also many of the very plants we now vilify as botanical bad boys – Japanese knotweed (*Reynoutria japonica*), hogweed (*Heracleum sphondylium*) and ragwort (*Jacobaea vulgaris*) to name but a few. To frame these plants as dangerous invaders – uncontrollable, aggressive and unwelcome – carries a deep irony. It also reveals an implicit preference for the native and the pure, drawing unsettling parallels to nationalistic ideologies. As Subramaniam notes, the language of invasion ecology mirrors the rhetoric of immigration: 'For anyone who is an immigrant, or who has experience of immigration, it's unmistakable'.

Dismantling these narratives and inherent biases is complex as they are deeply woven into our understanding of the world. But it's safe to say that inflammatory rhetoric, in any sphere, is both dangerous and inaccurate, serving only to reinforce stereotypes rather than engaging with facts. The deep unpicking of history required for true reckoning is often fraught and deeply uncomfortable, as the Black Lives Matter movement has made evident. However, many are finding ways to address these knotty socio-political narratives through a more personal lens – their own gardens.

In *Uprooting*, writer and gardener Marchelle Farrell explores the experience of creating a home in the countryside, in an environment shaped by systems that have historically excluded and oppressed people like her. Through cultivating her garden, Farrell confronts the uncomfortable entanglements of nature, race and colonial legacies, revealing how tending to the land can be both an act of healing and resistance. For gardener and writer Claire Ratinon, gardens have offered a way to reconnect with her Mauritian heritage. In her East Sussex garden, she deliberately cultivates plants native to Mauritius. She recalls her surprise at discovering a hibiscus growing in her garden and reflects on its significance: 'It didn't originate from this land, and yet it thrives here, and I think that's a really powerful image.' Creating a garden in East Sussex has deepened her connection to her cultural roots and challenged conventional notions of belonging and adaptability. 'I push my hands into the soil as an act of reclamation, of self-determination, of gesturing towards the possibility of establishing roots on my own terms because the land has chosen me and I have chosen her, no matter the prejudices of those who dwell here too.'

Choosing the land as a partner in protest is an alliance with a long and fruitful history. Pioneer nurseryman Johnny Appleseed (1774–1845) travelled across the American

← Clematis golden tiara grown by Alla Olkhovska in her garden in Kharkiv, Ukraine (pp.76-7).

73

Midwest, scattering apple seeds in a bid to reshape the landscape. By planting thousands of apple trees on public land, he not only challenged concepts of land ownership and food sovereignty, but also fuelled a booming cider market in the process. In 17th-century England, Gerrard Winstanley and the Diggers took their protest against land enclosure quite literally by plunging their spades into common land in a mission to make the world a 'common treasury'. Their efforts were met with violent oppression and eviction, yet their vision of environmental justice and ecological stewardship continues to resonate today, echoed in movements like Occupy, Extinction Rebellion and Just Stop Oil.

The Green Guerillas movement, known today as 'guerrilla gardening' (see Glossary), was born in 1970s New York, a city crumbling after years of economic stagnation, corruption and crime. Entire neighbourhoods had become ghost towns, abandoned and neglected. In response, Liz Christy and a team of activists began reclaiming these derelict spaces, one seed bomb at a time. But this wasn't just about beautification, it was a radical act of protest against urban neglect, economic inequality and environmental degradation. These guerrilla gardens became symbols of resistance, challenging ideas of land ownership, public space and community autonomy. More than just places to grow plants, they became fulcrums of ideas and linchpins of the community, hosting cultural events, educational programmes and serving as platforms for radical movements flourishing at the time.

In their brilliant book *The Garden Against Time: In Search of a Common Paradise,* Olivia Laing talks about communal gardens as everyday embodiments of a 'communal paradise'. These spaces offer a powerful counter-narrative to the history of colonial extraction embedded in many formal gardens - co-created landscapes where cultivation becomes an act of empowerment, reclaiming both land and cultural narratives. Ron Finley, the famed 'gangsta gardener' with a devoted following and a Masterclass series to match, brings this idea to life. By transforming slivers of land - from parking lots to highway verges - into thriving gardens, he combats food deserts in Los Angeles while cultivating more than just crops. He's growing economic freedom. 'To fight back, is to plant back,' he says. As in 1970s New York, the only way to fix the broken system is to take ownership of it.

Ownership is also a vital tool in the fight against isolation and estrangement, whether from our culture or the physical world around us. In San Francisco, garden design studio Terremoto co-created a garden at Café Ohlone to amplify Indigenous Ohlone culture and language. Plants carry stories - stories of Indigenous wisdom, traditional recipes and much-loved myths and legends. In South Africa, a newly planted circular Miyawaki forest (see Glossary) has reconnected Khoi First Nations people with their heritage, providing a physical space to commune, share vital traditions and ensure knowledge is celebrated for generations to come. Even in our own gardens we plant and grow things that connect us to our roots - a tree given as a wedding gift, a cutting from a grandmother's garden, or (whisper it) a plant smuggled back as a seed from a holiday.

In environments designed to punish and enforce isolation, gardens offer a route back to a world that feels out of reach. Prisons - deliberately devoid of green space as a means of control and dehumanization - become sites where gardening is a powerful act of resistance and hope. From London to Oregon and beyond, prison gardens serve as tools for rehabilitation, restoring dignity, rebuilding a sense of purpose and providing individuals with valuable skills for life on the outside. In the liminal space of a refugee camp, the simple act of planting - sometimes just a single seed in a plastic bottle - becomes a lifeline, a reminder that a world exists beyond the dystopian one at hand. Lalage Snow spent sixteen years as a war photographer, documenting with haunting beauty the gardens lovingly and tenderly cultivated against the impossibly bleak backdrop of war. In conflict zones around the world, she discovered an unstoppable human impulse to nurture and grow, from soldiers finding solace in creating miniature gardens in Camp Shorabak (formerly Camp Bastion) in Afghanistan to families in Jerusalem tending olive groves on contested, blood-soaked land.

Gardens are miniature worlds, places where we experiment, create and shape a vision of the world we long for, the one we have been separated from, or the one we wish to return to. Within them, we can gently untangle complex histories, co-create different futures and find the freedom that comes with cultivating a space that is truly our own.

An unused glasshouse at East Sutton →
Park women's prison in the UK is a site of
horticultural training for prisoners (pp.78-81).

Grow to generate an income and instill hope

Alla Olkhovska's Garden
Kharkiv, Ukraine
Alla Olkhovska

For generations, gardens have been a lifeline for Alla Olkhovska's family, whose history is tethered to the trauma of Ukraine's own struggles. Her great grandparents survived Stalin's famine, imprisonment and Siberian exile. It was only after her great-grandfather's wartime service that he was exonerated and granted a small a piece of land as a symbol of thanks for his contribution. On it, he built a house and planted an apple orchard, the fruits of which were famed and highly prized, earning him and his family an income for many years.

Now, in the throes of a different war, Olkhovska is once again turning to the land, using her garden to provide for her family under unimaginably difficult circumstances. 'Missile attacks often cause severe damage to the critical infrastructure,' she explains. 'We suffer long blackouts, which are especially tough during the winter. When there is no light, there is no heating or water. Due to power outages all the appliances burned out at my granny's place – her refrigerator, TV set, everything...We are often depressed and almost constantly

terrified.' But amidst the devastation, the garden is a constant source of hope.

Olkhovska grows clematis, a diverse and fascinating genus of flowering plants that offers constant delight. 'Many people believe that clematis is a vining plant, but the genus is extremely diverse and includes bushy varieties as well as dwarf ground covers [see Glossary].' Crucially, Olkhovska's passion for clematis has become a vital source of income. At the start of the war, she began photographing the flowers in her garden, which quickly gained traction on Instagram. Today, her family's income relies on seed orders, clematis eBook sales and Olkhovska's Patreon account, where she shares her gardening knowledge, courses and beautiful photographs of clematis, a fragile beauty defiantly thriving under the shadow of war. Her clematis have not only provided a financial lifeline but also a constant source of beauty and inspiration. 'Unfortunately, the war continues, but my small garden and all this work is what keeps me sane and helps my family survive. I can't even try to imagine what would happen if I didn't have my lovely garden.'

Learn to cultivate to thrive on the outside

The Glasshouse Botanics
East Sutton Park Prison, East Sutton, UK
Kali Hamerton-Stove (Co-Founder)

The reoffending rate for women leaving prison in the UK is alarmingly high: almost half are reconvicted within a year of being released. A toxic combination of high housing costs and low employment opportunities for women leaving prison means they are often 'set up to fail', says Kali Hamerton-Stove.

The Glasshouse Botanics offers an alternative future to women nearing the end of their prison sentence by providing horticultural training while in prison and employment opportunities upon release. Utilizing a previously neglected glasshouse at East Sutton Park Prison – once used to grow vegetables for the institution in bygone days – they learn to grow and nurture beautiful houseplants. These are sold through their website, the shop in Cranbrook, and a growing corporate gifting service.

This initiative equips women not only with the practical skills and tools needed to secure employment on release, but also with a renewed sense of purpose and self-worth. Learning new skills and spending time with nature plays a crucial role in rehabilitation. One woman who participated in the programme shared a striking observation: one of the most dehumanizing aspects of prison is the separation from nature through being locked in a cell for hours each day, with only brief spells in an exercise yard devoid of greenery. She recalled a moment when women fought over a single feather that had landed in the yard, so desperate were they for any sign of the natural world.

Working with plants in prison restores a vital sense of human dignity and allows women to begin life anew upon release, within a supportive community of fellow growers – and plants.

Explore injustice through making a garden

Solitary Gardens Project
Various locations, USA
jackie sumell

Nearly 100,000 incarcerated people in the United States endure indefinite solitary confinement every day, isolated in a 1.8 × 2.7-m (6 × 9-ft) concrete cell. The effects are devastating: alienation, paranoia, dehumanization and despair. The Solitary Gardens project is a collaborative project led by jackie sumell that applies the principles of prison abolition, permaculture and community power to facilitate unexpected exchanges between incarcerated people in solitary confinement and volunteers on the 'outside'. The initiative creates gardens the same size as a prison cell, designed by those in isolation and cultivated by proxies beyond the prison walls.

The projects are 'gardened' by the 'solitary gardeners' through letters and exchanges between incarcerated individuals and their proxies on the outside. 'Through growing almanacs, written and photographic exchanges, and occasional prison visits, we translate the imaginations of incarcerated individuals into the ground by cultivating the plants that they choose,' explains sumell. These Solitary Gardens serve as both a connection to the world outside the prison walls and powerful portraits of those held in the deepest reaches of the carceral system. The project is inspired by Herman Wallace, who was wrongly convicted of a crime he didn't commit and spent forty-one years in solitary confinement before his sentence was overturned, only to pass away three days after his release. At its core, the initiative seeks to expose the inhumanity of solitary confinement, inspire compassion and challenge systems of punishment and control, proving that 'nature – like hope, love and imagination – will ultimately triumph over the harm humans impose on ourselves and the planet'.

Unionize land workers for a fairer future

SALT (Solidarity Across Land Trades)
Various locations, UK
Claire Ratinon

For workers across land-based trades - whether on large industrial farms, country estates, nature reserves, small agroecological market gardens, or cut flower businesses – employment is often insecure, seasonal, informal and poorly paid. Many face discrimination, high levels of stress, and little to no job security or statutory benefits.

After years working in the sector, gardener and grower Claire Ratinon recognized a troubling pattern: here was an industry built on systemic low-level exploitation. Unpaid overtime, illegal 'traineeships', zero-hours contracts and a culture that glorified overwork and burnout were all commonplace, with workers expected to rely on sheer passion and goodwill to keep going.

SALT is a UK-based trade union created to represent workers in this sector, who, until now, have had no formal representation or legal protection, which is astonishing given how vital the sector is to our economy. The union aims to create a political consciousness among both workers and employers about the importance of workers' rights and solidarity among trades. 'It's also about getting people to understand themselves as workers, and to understand what their rights are in these spaces, and what it is to have those rights contravened,' explains Ratinon.

SALT also seeks to challenge the 'politically inconsistent' practices that progressive movements like agroecology have, whether unknowingly or out of necessity, inherited from mainstream agriculture and industrial farming. For Claire, this has prompted deep reflection on whether we are truly building a blueprint for the world we want to live in, and if we're not, what next?

This conversation is shaped by complex dynamics of class, money and power, all inextricably bound to an exploitative capitalist model. Before we start trying to create a new model that better serves people and planet, the problems embedded in the current system need careful unpicking and identifying. Thankfully, SALT is here to help us do just that.

Bridget Elworthy and Henrietta Courtauld aka The Land Gardeners

Dirt, black gold, soil – Bridget Elworthy and Henrietta Courtauld are obsessed with it, and have been for some time. It's the foundation of all life on Earth, and yet somehow we have paid very little attention to it, until now. That it has become a topic of conversation beyond the potting shed is likely to be thanks to Bridget and Henrietta's pioneering work as vocal advocates for the life-giving dirt beneath our feet. As garden designers, they know how vital good soil is to a garden that thrums with life. But its significance stretches far beyond beautiful borders. Soil underpins entire ecosystems – food, agriculture, farming, biodiversity and climate stability. Soil is one of the world's greatest carbon sinks, it provides 95% of the food we eat and is our best water filtration system. Yet according to the United Nations, up to 40% of the world's soil is already degraded due to intensive agricultural practices, chemical inputs and erosion. Bridget and Henrietta are on a mission to change this.

'What is wonderful about soil is that it is very empowering. We can all change our little bit of it,' Bridget tells me. And in doing so, we can begin to reverse some of the degradation we see across the globe. Bridget and Henrietta met at the school gate and quickly bonded over a shared passion for gardens, but more importantly, for soil health as the bedrock of any successful garden. For them, good soil health begins with good compost, a subject they've dedicated the last twelve years to obsessively refining.

Through endless trials and by experimenting with different composting methods (see Glossary), cover cropping with plants like phacelia to hold goodness in the soil early in the season (very effective), interplanting food crops with cut flowers and thinking about biodiversity at every turn, their work has paid off. At Wardington Manor, where they run their cut flower business, what was once a neglected walled garden now pulses with life, with soil that is dense and rich with protozoa, fungi and microbes. Based on their research and hands-on experience, they have developed their own special brew of hyper-potent 'Climate Compost' inoculum, supercharged

with microbes to get your soil humming, as well as a Gardener's Tonic – a biodynamic preparation combining valerian, oak bar and other hedgerow botanicals, to give both plants and soil an extra boost.

But Bridget and Henrietta now have their sights set on a broader horizon. It's no longer just the soil in our gardens they want to improve, but soil all over the world. Working with the Organic Research Centre (ORC), they have begun scientific trials to test different soil improvement methods. The goal is to work with farmers to identify which composting methods available are most effective at improving soil biology. This information will be added to their 'Map of Hope' – a vast global, digital network of farmers and gardeners around the world, practising good soil health. The goal is to collate and disseminate the science on this growing field of research, so that people all over the world can participate. 'It can feel overwhelming,' they acknowledge – there's so much information out there, and not all methods are practical for every scale or context. Some require specialist equipment, others aren't suitable for large operations. The Map of Hope is designed to cut through that noise, becoming a trusted resource where farmers, home growers and community gardeners alike can find what works and feel empowered to improve their own patch of earth.

In February 2025, Bridget and Henrietta curated an exhibition at Somerset House in London titled *Soil: The World at Our Feet*. It was a novel and timely exploration of a subject that is all too often confined to the horticultural or agricultural margins. The exhibition explored soil through a wide-ranging and imaginative lens, bringing together artists, filmmakers, mycologists, designers and writers to explore its richness, both literally and metaphorically. 'What was wonderful to see was how many people wanted to come – and people of all ages,' says Bridget. Its success is emblematic of a broader shift. People want to reconnect with the Earth, whether through floristry, gardening, or growing their own food. People are beginning to understand that everything is connected, from our vegetable patches to global harvests, and at the heart of it all lies the soil.

Garden to restore dignity

Oregon State Penitentiary Garden
Salem, Oregon, USA
Kurisu/Incarcerated men

The healing garden at Oregon State Penitentiary is remarkable for many reasons, not least because it was co-designed by the incarcerated men in this maximum-security prison alongside renowned Japanese landscape designer Hoichi Kurisu.

Previously a neglected piece of land, the project began when the men were asked how they might improve it. An incarcerated member of the Asian Pacific Family Club suggested a Japanese garden with a koi pond. Having no access to the outside world or the internet, a visitor to the prison managed to find a phone number for a Japanese garden design company. From a shared pay phone, a couple of inmates cold-called the firm and pitched their idea. By sheer chance, they had contacted one of the country's leading Japanese landscape designers. More remarkably, Kurisu was a man who believed that those in prison had as much right to a garden as anyone else.

Prison life is defined by denial, of freedom, comfort, purpose, human touch and nature. Many of the men involved in the project were serving multiple life sentences and hadn't set foot outside for thirty years. The impact of the garden on their wellbeing, dignity and sense of hope cannot be overstated.

More than 200 imprisoned men worked together to build it, an act of collective transformation that kickstarted a healing process so profound no one could have predicted it. Men who had previously lived in isolation, unable to integrate safely with the rest of the prison population, found peace and calm within the garden. Prison environments are hostile places where vulnerability must be hidden at all costs. However, the culture of the garden was different – nurturing plants and tending to the landscape they had built took precedence over the toxic hierarchies inside. For some, rediscovering nature after decades of deprivation was a deeply moving experience, unlocking a sense of purpose and connection that traditional rehabilitation programmes had failed to achieve.

This garden is now a blueprint for a more compassionate approach to justice, one that prioritizes collaboration, respect and the healing power of nature as key components in successful rehabilitation. It raises profound questions about how justice is defined and what it truly means to restore a person's humanity.

Grow plants that connect you to home

Garden of the Month
Various locations, Kurdistan
Lemon Tree Trust

Creativity, flair and innovative planting ideas might not be the first things you associate with refugee camps. Yet, across nine camps in Kurdistan, displaced gardeners compete each month for the coveted title of Garden of the Month. What began with just a few seeds has, over the past decade, blossomed into a thriving network of gardening clubs, prizes and community projects, thanks to the Lemon Tree Trust. These initiatives provide much-needed pride, joy and wellbeing in stark and uncertain times.

What gardeners choose to grow is often revelatory. It's not just about food or sustenance, but about beauty, memory and identity. A rose that reminds them of home, snapdragons like the ones in their grandmother's garden – such choices speak to a deep longing for connection. The need for beauty becomes even more urgent when life as you know it has been uprooted. People forced to flee war often arrive at camps with nothing but the essentials, unsure of how long they will stay. In these dehumanizing environments, growing a garden is an act of resilience, restoring a sense of place, belonging and dignity, building hope and providing a much-needed creative outlet. 'My garden is proof that I still have something to give, that I am still creative. And when I've finished gardening, I feel like I have the world in my hand,' says Khaled Ismael, a refugee from Syria.

Initially, the Lemon Tree Trust simply provided seeds, enabling people to start growing. Now, they are creating community gardens, fostering shared purpose and connection in these extraordinarily dislocated places. Women come together to grow herbs for teas and reminisce about home. Children play, learn about growing and find moments of normalcy. The gardens become vibrant social hubs – spaces for cooking, relaxing and reclaiming a sense of everyday life. These are simple, familiar activities that we often take for granted, but for thousands living indefinitely in no-man's lands, they are profound acts of hope and restoration.

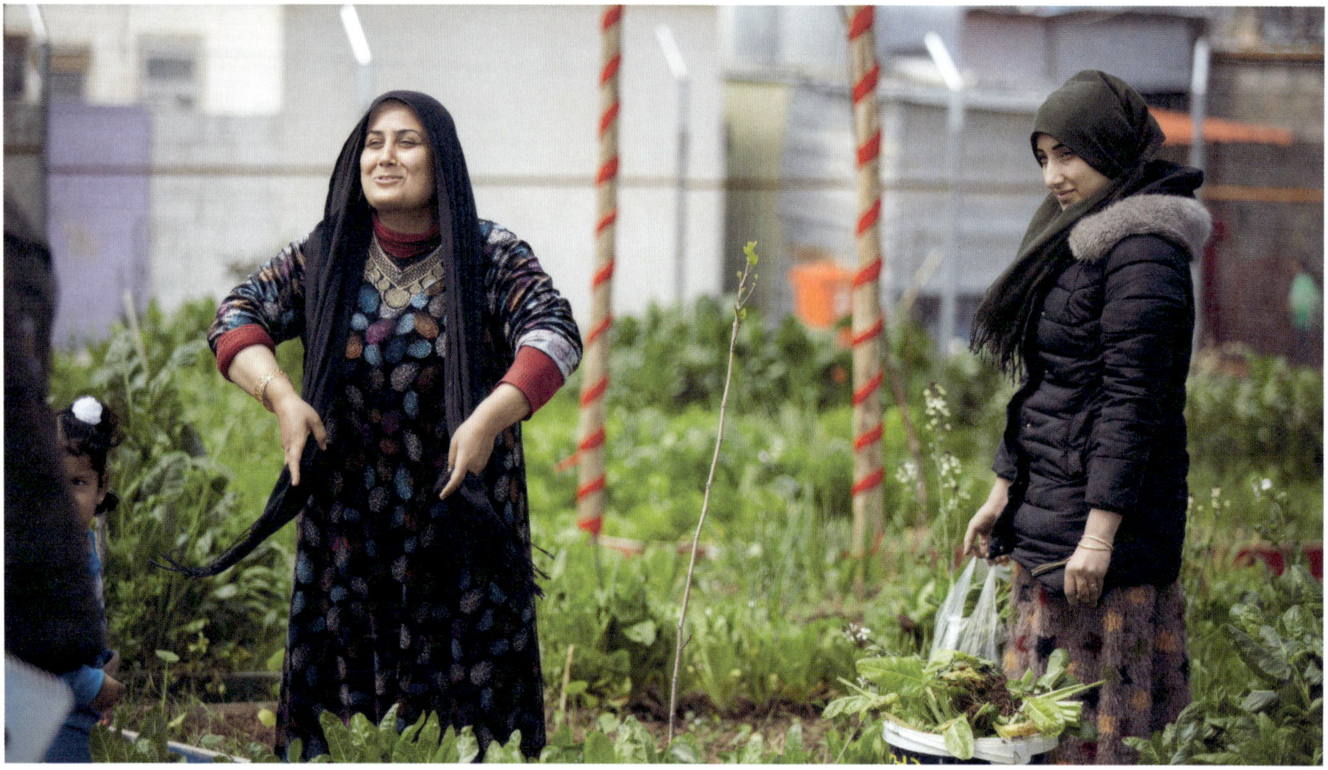

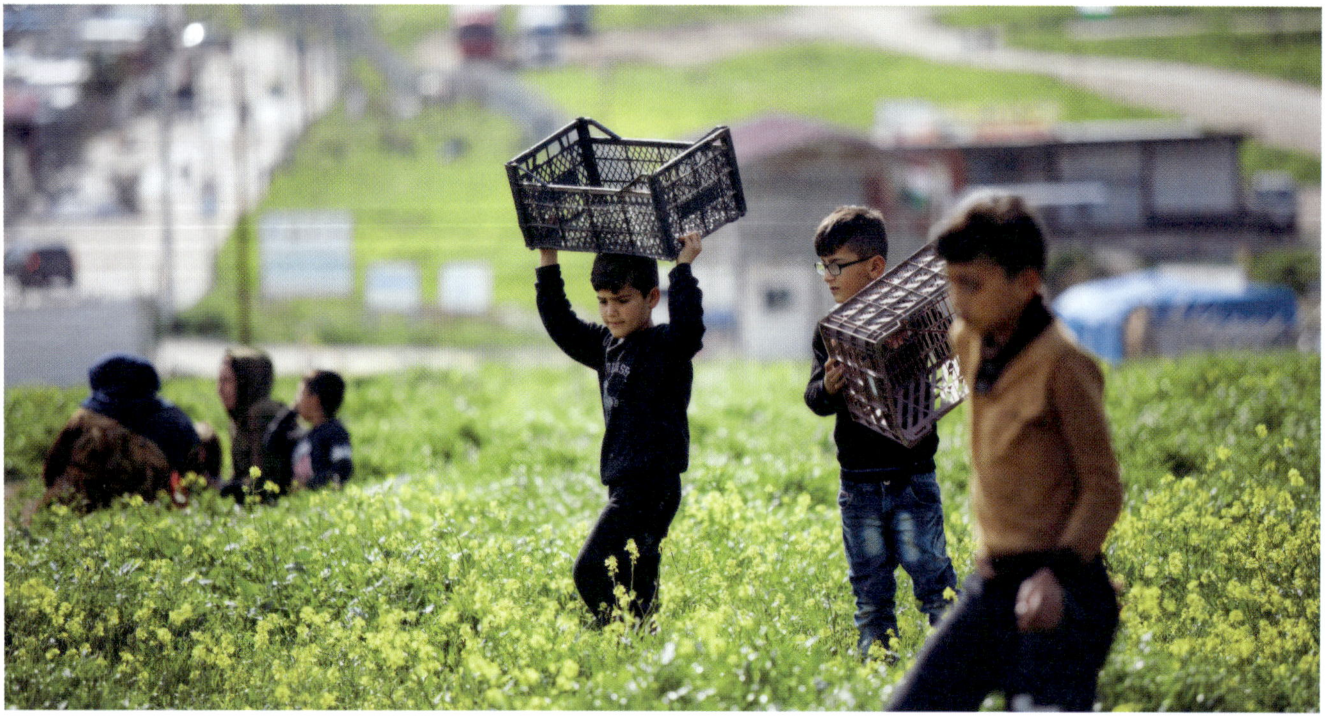

Plant to restore resilience in the throes of war

Seeds of Resilience
Various locations, Gaza
Bisan Okasha

An often-overlooked consequence of war is the total decimation of nature. Amid the lives lost and the homes destroyed, gardens and green spaces are wiped off the map, along with the places where people gather, grow and sustain cultural traditions passed down through generations. In Gaza, food security has always been precarious, as has a sense of self-determination. Creating gardens offers answers to both.

Seeds of Resilience is an initiative led by a small group of young people in Gaza, including architecture student Bisan Okasha. Despite the physical and emotional toll of war, Bisan is determined to be part of a solution. The enormity of rebuilding amid war can feel overwhelming, but planting seedlings – tangible signs of life, renewal and security – offers a way forwards for the country. Vegetable crops not only provide essential nutrition but also symbolize hope and agency in a place where both are systematically denied.

The challenges are immense: sourcing seeds, getting access to water and surviving in an environment where there is a constant threat to safety. But, as Bisan explains, 'for a Palestinian to care for their land, to find something that reassures them that every material loss can be recovered, to remain connected to their land, nurture it, plant in it and reap the fruits of their own labour – this is a powerful act of resilience and hope'. Through these gardens, Bisan and her team are sowing more than just crops. They are cultivating dignity, renewal and a deep-rooted defiance against forces that seek to deny them their basic civil liberties.

Kalpana Arias Technologist, Guerrilla Gardener and Founder of Nowadays, a social enterprise advocating for contact with nature

Technology is often seen as the enemy – part of the problem, not the solution. The headlines are swamped with stories about the damage social media does to young minds, about childhoods lost to scrolling and Snapchat. But what if technology could actually bring us closer to nature? What might that look like? Could digital tools help us rekindle our relationship with the natural world?

Kalpana grew up in Bogotá, Colombia, surrounded by lush, deep green valleys and a culture imbued with Indigenous wisdom and respect for the living world. Some of her earliest memories are of her mother teaching her to talk to plants, beginning a life-long belief in the wisdom of the wild. In her early teens, a move to Houston, Texas, opened up new horizons, immersing her in a new kind of jungle: one of concrete and screens, education and technology.

Today, via her social enterprise Nowadays, Kalpana is dedicated to helping people reconnect with nature, and uses technology as a tool to help them do that. The need for democratizing access to green space became apparent to Kalpana during lockdown, when access to a garden proved vital for so many of us. At the same time, she was learning to code and program, and organically these two worlds came together. Instead of seeing them as opposing forces, Kalpana began to see how technology and the natural world could be allies.

For Kalpana, there are parallels between the Indigenous wisdom she was immersed in as a child, and technology; both, she believes, are a type of collective consciousness. 'Within Indigenous culture we talk a lot about the dreamworld and the power of the collective dream. Technology is like that, a tool for creation.' She believes it is possible to build technology that serves both people *and* the planet. We are currently suffering from a kind of 'generational amnesia' about the natural world. Knowledge, stories, myths and skills are being lost. But technology, she argues, could be used to help us 'fight against the system that's luring us into this sleep – a partner in creating a greener world'.

So, what does this actually look like? 'We have started working with different emerging technologies like AI (Artificial Intelligence), VR (Virtual Reality) and gamified nature apps to create a space where we can explore how tech can create this vision of nature that we can all feel but is sometimes hard to imagine – we are using the master's tools to destroy the master's house.' The result is Glitch, a platform using AI, machine learning and AR (Augmented Reality) to help us imagine and build a greener, more interconnected future (see page 206).

Nowadays hosts 'plant fiction' workshops for brands around the world – most recently for Apple, at their flagship store in London's Covent Garden, where customers were challenged to reimagine their local greenery using an iPad. But can simply imagining a greener world bring it into being? Kalpana believes it can. Our current disconnection from nature is now so systemic, so entrenched, that many of us have no real living memory of what it means to be in harmony with nature. Furnishing us with the tools to reconnect is the essential first step. It's a type of 're-indigenization' – a return to ancestral ways of knowing, to spark the imagination and energy needed to shape a different future.

There's an inherent tension between nature and tech, but increasingly, technology and gardening are becoming intertwined and finding unlikely synergies, shaping how people grow, maintain and connect with plants. On a practical level technology can enable more efficient and sustainable gardening through tools like soil sensors, automated irrigation systems, plant health apps, and even AI-driven design platforms. At the same time, this relationship can create tension: while technology offers convenience, many turn to gardening as a way to unplug and reconnect with the natural world. By outsourcing the slow and gentle observation that gardening demands of us, are we missing the point?

Kalpana cautions against turning away from it entirely. There is huge scope for harnessing tech as a force for good, one that can teach us to recognize bird calls, help us identify unknown plants or constellations in the sky. It can serve as a bridge, deepening curiosity, lowering barriers to participation and filling the gaps in our knowledge that have appeared over the last generation of increasingly urban living. Tech is, and always has been, a mirror of society - good, bad and ugly. It's our responsibility to harness its power for good. For Kalpana and her team, that is reconnecting humans with nature.

Plant orchards to build community and food security

The Orchard Project
Various locations, UK
Rowena Ganguli and Carina Millstone (Founders)

Community cohesion is the bedrock of a healthy society. Yet, persistent structural inequalities, inadequate health provision and low social integration in parts of the UK are leading to fractured communities vulnerable to extremism, crime and ill health. Time and again, research shows that access to green space strengthens community ties and that shared activities in those spaces deepen the benefits.

The Orchard Project is a nationwide initiative dedicated to planting orchards in the heart of urban communities, working with local hubs to design, create and maintain them. It also offers the UK's only accredited course in managing community orchards. Unlike traditional vegetable gardens, which require intensive labour and dedicated land, orchards are a more sustainable and equitable food system, providing free organic produce in areas experiencing high food insecurity.

Beyond food production, urban orchards serve as rich, biodiverse spaces that bring people together. They offer a natural setting for shared experiences – harvest festivals, Apple Day, Blossom Day, jam-making workshops – fostering pride and connection across social and ethnic divides. By nurturing these spaces, The Orchard Project cultivates not just fruit, but stronger, more resilient communities.

Stabilize a fractured city by sowing hope on abandoned land

Green Guerillas
New York, USA
Amos Taylor and others

Guerrilla gardening, although often thought of as a modern movement, actually took root in 1970s New York, born out of the city's descent into urban decay. A fiscal crisis, political corruption and the ensuing 'white flight' left entire neighbourhoods abandoned, fuelling homelessness, vandalism and drug use, especially in lower-income areas.

'It was a form of civil disobedience,' recalls Amos Taylor, one of the founders of Green Guerillas, the grassroots organization credited with sparking the global community gardening movement. What began with just a few sunflower seeds scattered into trash-filled intersections and window boxes perched on the ledges of derelict buildings soon became a rallying cry for reclaiming urban spaces. The idea exploded

and soon pockets of land all over the city were being transformed into community gardens. These were spaces not just for growing food, but for cultivating connection, resilience and hope.

Today the legacy of the Green Guerillas lives on, not only in the 600+ community gardens across New York City, but in every seed bomb and reclaimed urban plot around the world. What started as a small act of defiance has blossomed into a global movement, empowering communities to take ownership of their land, build food security and forge social bonds. Whether in New York or New Delhi, a community garden is more than just green space – it's a place where people can kneel down together and cultivate something greater than themselves.

Create a garden that tells a story about your culture

Café Ohlone
San Francisco, USA
Terremoto

Despite progress in recognizing the sovereignty of Indigenous peoples, Native communities in America still face discrimination, high poverty rates and limited access to healthcare and education. The pressure to assimilate into society, environmental degradation of ancestral lands and cultural appropriation have all contributed to the gradual erosion of Indigenous culture and language.

mak-'amham, or Café Ohlone, is an organization dedicated to preserving the Ohlone language and culture. In collaboration with Terremoto, the café's garden serves as an extension of this mission – a series of interconnected spaces that guide visitors from the 'outside' world through to one that is fully Ohlone, 'a sovereign nation unto itself,' as Story Wiggins, partner at Terremoto, describes.

The garden is planted with species of deep cultural significance – plants the Ohlone people have historically used for food, medicine or shelter, such as wild ginger, Pacific blackberry and hummingbird sage. In Ohlone culture, plants have voices, a belief brought to life through Café Ohlone's singing trees: seven native trees planted with recordings of native speakers, filling the garden with song.

At the far end of the café is a table reserved for elders and members of the Ohlone community, a revered space surrounded by symbols and stories of their heritage. The garden itself is testament to the survival of Ohlone culture, a vehicle for greater visibility and as founder Vincent Medina puts it, a vital reminder that 'the Ohlone people are alive and well'.

Reframe the idea of weeds and rethink beauty

Campo Sucio
Contemporary Art Space, Montevideo, Uruguay
Teresa Puppo/Alejandro O'Neill

In Uruguay, the term *campo sucio* – meaning 'dirty field' – is used in rural areas to describe land overrun with *chircas* and other so-called 'undesirable' plants, rendering it unsuitable for grazing or extractive farming. But these 'weeds' are, in fact, native trees and shrubs that support a thriving ecosystem of wildlife and biodiversity. Considered obstacles to progress, they are often destroyed using toxic herbicides to make way for monoculture farming.

This pattern of erasing native landscapes in favour of commercial agriculture echoes colonial histories worldwide – where domination of land, people and culture follows a similar narrative. The language of 'native' versus 'non-native', of 'invasive threats', has long been used not just in ecology but in conversations about immigration, belonging and power. Campo Sucio, a collective project led by artist and writer Teresa Puppo and Alejandro O'Neill, challenges these perceptions by reclaiming native flora as an essential part of Uruguay's natural and cultural identity. Their first public project at Montevideo's Contemporary Art Space is an installation that transforms a former detention centre into a space for reflection, learning and community engagement. By redefining native plants often dismissed as weeds, Teresa and Alejandro have created a garden showcasing species rarely viewed through an ornamental lens in Uruguay. In doing so, they promote 'a new relationship with nature in the city', one that 'rethinks beauty standards and fosters an inclusive perspective on the landscape'. Through this living, evolving work of art, Campo Sucio is shifting perceptions of how we understand the landscape and reshaping ideas of beauty.

Plant a forest garden to address inequality

District Six
Cape Town, South Africa
SUGi

In Cape Town, the legacy of apartheid can be mapped across the city in the abundance (or not) of green spaces. Areas demarcated as white-only were cleared, and people who lived there were forcibly removed and displaced to make way for segregated green spaces. In District Six, a Miyawaki forest garden is now growing as a symbol of renewal and reconciliation after a traumatic past. It was planted by SUGi, an ecosystem restoration organization specializing in urban greening, whose secret weapon is the Miyawaki method – a rapid reforestation technique implemented by a global network of forest makers.

For Aghmad Gamieldien, the forest maker who led this project, the site holds deep personal significance. 'This forest resonates deeply with me on a personal level, as it holds memories and connections to my family, and indeed many others who were displaced from this area during the apartheid era.' Planted beside a school, the garden provides an outdoor learning space and a vital connection to nature, something many children in District Six would otherwise have to travel an hour to access. 'Inequality is a reality in Cape Town and South Africa. It's the most unequal place in the world, not just in terms of wealth but also access to green space. Green areas weren't created for Black people and other people of colour,' Aghmad explains. This forest garden is more than just a much-needed resource for the young people living in District Six. It is a step towards restoring balance – both socially and ecologically – a powerful act of environmental justice and a timely response to the legacy of apartheid and its enduring scars.

Build self-reliance with urban food sovereignty and spark a movement

Gangsta Gardening
Los Angeles, USA
Ron Finley

'Plant some money' is Ron Finley's rallying cry. While this literally means 'grow some veg', the deeper message here is one of empowerment, stressing the importance of equipping yourself with the skills and knowledge to be self-reliant and independent of the systems that constrain you.

In LA, these systems have created food deserts – areas where access to fresh, healthy food is severely limited or non-existent. In some neighbourhoods, a fresh tomato might be a forty-five-minute drive away. Across the USA, an estimated 23.5 million people live in food deserts, disproportionately affecting African American and Latin American communities. Limited access to nutritious food has led to higher obesity rates and a whole host of other serious health issues, with a knock-on affect on mental health and wellbeing.

Determined to challenge this reality, Ron began planting vegetables in neglected patches of land in 2010. Authorities pounced on him for gardening without a permit, but he fought back, and won. His defiance sparked a movement, inspiring a growing army of green activists demanding the right to garden and grow. Today, Finley's influence extends far beyond the food deserts of LA. Gangsta Gardening has evolved into a global phenomenon, feeding neighbourhoods and empowering communities all over the world to build their own resilience and strength – through gardens. His message remains the same: 'Go out and do something. Change your world. People like to call me the Black guy that grows food on the street, but I'm the guy that's been able to change people's lives all over the world because of a simple message: gardens equal freedom.'

NO

URISH

Our connection to the land is intimately tied to its ability to nourish us. For thousands of years, as nomads, we roamed freely, gathering nature's bounty. Every civilization since has reinforced this bond – until now. Today, we are entangled in the agro-industrial complex, a system of mind-boggling complexity that prioritizes profit over people and the planet. Global supply chains have become faceless and disruptive, the systems feeding us are increasingly toxic – both literally and metaphorically – and our relationship with what we eat and where it comes from has never been more distorted. We produce more than ever, yet we have never been so poorly nourished. Where did it all go wrong?

The toxic triple helix of urbanization, capitalism and industrialization – once lauded as the hallmark of progress – has left deep scars on our ability to meet even our most basic needs. By 2050, seven in ten of the global population will live in cities. Over the past fifty years, the challenge of feeding growing urban populations has been seized by corporate conglomerates, promising efficiency and convenience while tightening their grip on the global food system. As populations explode, land values skyrocket. The idea of using prime real estate to grow vegetables locally when there are cities to build seems laughably quaint. Especially when we can outsource food production to out-of-town industrial feedlots, or faraway plantations, depleting natural resources and destroying rainforests in the process. Yet this system isn't feeding us, it's making us sick. Ultra-processed foods, now dietary staples, are increasingly linked to obesity, type 2 diabetes, cardiovascular disease and various cancers. Progress, it seems, has come at a heavy price.

But there is a palpable shift – having entered this dystopian dining room, we are awakening to the error of our ways. All over the world, people are seeking a more direct route from farm to table. Waiting lists for oversubscribed allotments suggest a growing appetite for homegrown food across the Global North. In the UK alone, a staggering 170,000 people are waiting for the opportunity to grow their own vegetables, and could be waiting for decades. The tradition of common land for the cultivation of vegetables and grazing livestock has a long history. The Enclosure Acts in the UK, beginning in the 17th century, systematically erased common land, stripping the working classes of their ability to feed themselves. In response, allotments of land were attached to tenant cottages and 'field gardens' were designated for the landless poor. The 1908 Small Holdings and Allotments Act imposed a legal obligation on councils to provide land for residents to grow their own food, an obligation that technically remains in force today, though in practice, securing a plot may take the best part of a generation.

Other attempts to integrate pastoral life into urban planning emerged with the garden city movement, inspired by Ebenezer Howard's 1898 publication, *Garden Cities of To-morrow*. In his vision, town and country would blend harmoniously in a healthy self-sufficient balance of residential, agricultural and industrial land use. Garden city principles gained traction in the early 20th century, shaping post-war developments and influencing colonial and post-colonial capitals. Today, they are experiencing a revival, albeit primarily at an intellectual level.

Garden cities might provide solutions for new housing, but how can their principles be retrofitted to the densely packed metropolises where 60% of the world's population now lives? Urban farming – finding novel ways to grow high-quality food in scarce pockets of inner-city land – has become a galvanizing mission for policy makers, governments and citizens alike. Frustrated by inaction, guerrilla gardening collectives have grasped the proverbial nettle and are greening cities one vacant parking lot at a time. In Taipei, this has dovetailed with a flourishing permaculture movement; in Rio de Janeiro's favelas, it's taking root in underserved communities like Manguinhos.

In a less anarchic fashion, urban farming is also advancing through precision technology, opening up new opportunities in spaces once considered unsuitable for agriculture. In Paris, urban farms are carpeting rooftops; in Malaysia, hydroponic systems are generating ten times more produce than traditional methods, while vertical farms are quite literally conjuring productive land out of thin air.

At the not-so new-fangled end of the spectrum, growers are turning to time-honoured and ancient techniques to combat the challenges climate change presents to achieving a decent harvest. In Bangladesh, where flooding can submerge land for months on end, floating productive gardens offer a lifeline. Meanwhile, on Exmoor in the UK, Korean fermentation methods are being deployed to replenish nutrient-depleted soils.

← **Tomatoes grow in the Nature Urbaine rooftop garden in Paris (pp.128-9).**

Traditional techniques are also being used to tackle food scarcity, an increasingly pressing concern in a world of geopolitical flux and global pandemics. Food forests, a staple of Indigenous communities for centuries, particularly in tropical regions, mimic natural ecosystems with diverse, layered planting, making them resilient and abundant. In New Zealand, Roimata Food Commons uses them as a more equitable way of tackling food poverty. And because they're much less labour-intensive, once established they're available to a wider demographic who may not have the luxury of time or space to cultivate using traditional methods. In Croatia, Bogata Šuma has expanded the concept into an edible landscape that fosters both communal living, and social as well as nutritional nourishment.

Restoring a healthier food system starts with revitalizing food education. Two decades after celebrity chef Jamie Oliver exposed the dismal state of British school meals – making the turkey twizzler infamous – meaningful change remains elusive. However, bridging the gap between plants and plates is a key piece of the jigsaw puzzle. Food-growing charities such as GROW are pioneering a hyper-local agroecological model of farm to fork, by growing produce for a North London school on site. In Kenya, reinstating small gardens of heritage varieties of local crops – and the knowledge, culture and recipes that come with them – is key to the fight against monocrops and industrial agriculture.

Better quality food and equitable access to it are at the heart of so many social issues. Where and how we grow our food is vital to our health and that of the planet. Thankfully, from Parisian rooftops to underground car parks and everything in between, innovative green-fingered growers are finding a way.

Curved raised beds grow the ingredients for the Chalet de la Forêt restaurant in Belgium (pp.124–5). →

Plant a food forest to make gardening more accessible

Roimata Food Commons
Christchurch, New Zealand
Michael Reynolds

Michael Reynolds started Roimata Food Commons to challenge the 'sweat-equity' dynamic (earning an interest in the garden in return for labour) that underpins many productive community gardens. While the idea of working in the garden to earn a share of the produce may sound fair, it unintentionally favours those who have the time, health and knowledge to participate, leaving those who don't – often those who need it most – locked out of the system. Creating a community garden as a food forest goes some way to combatting this imbalance. Unlike traditional raised beds, a food forest is a more complex and diverse planting system that mimics natural ecosystems with multiple layers – ground cover, shrubs, understory and canopy – where every plant is edible. By growing like this, you are not only making much better use of the land and creating variegated and complex habitats, but you're facilitating a different kind of participation. There is far less labour involved as plants tend to be perennials rather than labour-intensive annual crops and 'harvesting' feels more like foraging, with people taking what they need when they need it, rather than gathering large crops at designated times. It's also a much less intimidating, more naturalistic and immersive environment for those unfamiliar with growing or seeking solace and comfort.

This gentler approach has allowed Reynolds to shift the concept of a community garden towards one that genuinely serves those who need it most, embodying the true spirit of a Food Commons.

Look after your soil to look after your gut

Root Project
Oare Valley, Exmoor, UK
Caroline Duval/Hadyn Potts

Farm-to-table is now a well-established concept, but soil-to-gut perhaps less so. In the wild depths of the Oare Valley in Exmoor National Park, husband-and-wife team Caroline and Hadyn are developing a truly holistic approach to nourishment. Here, the biology of the land and our guts are deemed of equal worth, inextricably linked in an ancient evolutionary dance that modern food systems have all but forgotten. Not all vegetables are created equal. Nutrient-depleted soils, stripped of essential mycorrhizal networks by industrial farming techniques, yield lacklustre crops that offer little nutritional value. In turn, they do little for our health, particularly our gut microbiota, which is increasingly recognized as the engine room not just for our digestive health, but also for our immune systems and brain function. Healthy and rich gut microbiota comes from equally healthy and rich soils.

To enrich their land, Caroline and Hadyn work with saprophytic fungi to stimulate soil fungal activity, grow microbial tinctures and teas that are intimately connected to their land, and practice Korean fermentation techniques learned from soil expert Joshua Sparkes, who trained in Korea. These methods boost microbial activity in both their soil and their own guts. More recently, they have introduced fermented indigo dyeing to their practice, which not only imbues the fabric with antibacterial properties but also benefits conditions like eczema. The leftover dye is fed back into the compost – mirroring a Japanese practice that even helps clean up the rivers – creating, as Caroline puts it, 'another loop in the gut/soil health web'. By reviving these time-honoured farming techniques, Caroline and Hadyn are nourishing themselves, their community and the soil they rely on.

Reinvent formal layouts to make growing vegetables more engaging

Le Chalet de la Forêt
Brussels, Belgium
Erik Dhont

At the height of the season, productive gardens are a gorgeous feast for the senses – abundant, humming with pollinators and deeply wholesome. The classic *potager*, or kitchen garden, is both romantic and practical, with a series of beds laid out in a neat grid to allow for easy tending and harvesting. In grand houses and country estates these gardens are often walled to create sheltered conditions for growing and positioned away from the more traditionally decorative parts of the garden as a working space for staff only. But today they are often proudly flaunted, showcased as proof of one's farm-to-table credentials.

For Belgian two-star chef, Pascal Devalkeneer, the *potager* is a fundamental part of his creative process, allowing him to potter in the garden and craft his menus based on whatever looks most delicious that morning. When he took up his post

at Le Chalet de la Forêt, he enlisted the landscape architect Erik Dhont to reimagine the humble *potager* kitchen garden in the same way he, as a chef, elevates humble ingredients into a changing menu of masterpieces each day with the artistry he brings to the plate. The traditional rectilinear grid was disposed of and replaced by a series of sweeping organic curves. The beds, which are raised almost a metre off the ground, deliver both practical working height and dramatic visual impact, while creating a feeling of order. Towering forests of fennel, frothy clouds of aromatic herbs together with sculptural vegetables generate a sense of immersive abundance. The result is an undulating constellation of raised beds that are a joy to wander among, for chef Devalkeneer and his lucky guests alike.

Adapt your technique to use what you have in abundance

Floating Gardens

Ganges, Brahmaputra and Meghna rivers, Bangladesh

Various/Community Food System

For low-income families living in Bangladesh, a country where nearly 80% of the land is occupied by the alluvial plains of the Ganges, Brahmaputra and Meghna rivers, land is both scarce and vital. Increasingly volatile monsoons mean a great deal of the available land is submerged for as much as eight months of the year. Even when the floods recede, land is waterlogged, making cultivation of vegetables impossible. Floating gardens offer a solution, allowing families to grow vegetables hydroponically even during the monsoons, and thereby reducing their vulnerability to climate change.

These floating beds are created by gathering water hyacinth, duckweed or paddy stubs, mixing them with silt and cow dung, and weaving them into rafts. Seedlings are then planted in these floating 'beds'. Crops like bitter gourd, squash, okra, red amaranth, spinach and aubergine all thrive on these floating island beds, which simply rise and fall with the swelling rivers, and are less susceptible to plant diseases and weeds compared to traditional terrestrial gardens.

Not only do they provide valuable crops and strengthen food security for the families who tend them, but these floating gardens also serve as shelters for poultry and small cattle during the monsoon season and offer fishing opportunities. At the end of their life cycle, the floating farms can be broken down and repurposed as mulch or used for growing winter crops such as cabbage, turnips and cauliflower. They have proved so effective in meeting the needs of rural families in Bangladesh that they are now being trialled in other regions facing similar challenges, including Myanmar.

Use aeroponics to unlock rooftop growing space

Nature Urbaine
Paris, France
Pascal Hardy (Founder)

A vertical, closed-loop, pesticide-free farming system is taking over Paris's rooftops. With over a hundred hectares of rooftop farm, it is the largest system of its kind in Europe. One standout example is Nature Urbaine, a 6,000 m² (19,685 ft²) rooftop garden, made up of allotments and productive growing beds, supplying the city's top restaurants with fresh herbs, fruit and vegetables.

By combining hydroponics and aeroponics, Nature Urbaine grows produce far more efficiently than if they were to use traditional methods. These systems are lighter in weight and have a reduced physical footprint, as plants grow vertically, maximizing every inch. The result is not only a hyper-efficient food production system, but it also carpets Paris's otherwise barren rooftops with thousands of square metres of carbon-thirsty planting.

Parisians sign up through an allotment system, which also gives them access to growing advice via the on-site growing teams and a series of seasonal growing workshops. There's also an events space and a veg-box scheme, serving local businesses and creating a community of like-minded people in a busy cosmopolitan city. The result is a hyper-local, seasonal food system, where people living in the buzz of a city can enjoy the benefits of farm-to-table eating.

Rebecca McMackin Ecological Landscape Designer and Horticulturalist

Rebecca McMackin's 'ecologically obsessed' approach to planting design is both wildly effective and extremely infectious – so much so that her TED Talk, *Let Your Garden Grow Wild*, has notched up over a million views. In it, she discusses the strategies she and her team implemented during her time as Director of Horticulture at Brooklyn Bridge Park (see page 30), a project that transformed a post-industrial site into an eighty-five-acre haven for wildlife complete with drifting clouds of monarch butterflies and nights ablaze with fireflies. These gardens are 'extravagantly beautiful', but their value goes far beyond aesthetics; they also provide a vital 'habitat for plant populations, wildlife communities and soil organisms' alike. It's a win-win model, but not one we're all following. Not all gardens are created equal, in fact some are near ecological deserts, delivering almost no benefit to wildlife populations at all, despite many being in critical danger of extinction. Gardening in a way that supports wildlife and boosts biodiversity isn't complicated, but it is also not the norm. Rebecca is on a mission to change that.

'My hope is to connect us to the world around us. To introduce people to the non-human members of their community,' says Rebecca. 'Especially in cities, people can forget about birds and flowers and butterflies. It's a tragedy that I believe leads to immeasurable damage.' A key piece of the jigsaw is planting native species. These are plants that have co-evolved with local wildlife over thousands of years, forming vital links in the ecosystem. When these links are severed, we break a fragile and complex system of co-dependency leaving many insects and animals without food or habitat. By planting native plants and embracing other simple ecologically sound practices – like leaving fallen leaves in place or letting our lawns grow long – we not only gain 'a front-row seat to the wonders of the natural world,' but also take meaningful action in reversing the biodiversity crisis.

Tweaking how we garden, by choosing a diverse palette of native plants, can have a dramatic effect, creating vital habitats for pollinators, birds and insects, which in turn helps to reverse local biodiversity loss. Eliminating pesticides and chemical fertilizers allows beneficial organisms to thrive and supports healthier soil ecosystems. Even small gardens, when managed with biodiversity in mind, can form ecological networks that strengthen resilience against the biodiversity crisis.

Biodiverse environments are not just vital for wildlife, they're essential for human wellbeing too. 'Ecological gardening has the ability to repair something broken within so many of us – the isolation and loneliness that can come from living in this often callous world,' says Rebecca. In her opinion, everyone has a right to live in a healthy and verdant environment, and 'public gardens in cities are a big part of making that a reality'. A research paper in Philadelphia found that when an abandoned lot was cleaned up and planted, gun crime in the surrounding neighbourhood dropped by 29%. Another in Helsinki found that by giving kids access to healthy soils, their immune system function skyrocketed in a matter of weeks. With a growing body of evidence showing the profound impact of green spaces on mental and physical health, access to nature should be considered a basic human right. For Rebecca, public gardens are key to making that vision a reality.

Alongside her work at Brooklyn Bridge Park, Rebecca has proven that ecological planting has a place in other unconventional settings too, most notably at the entrance to Brooklyn Museum. Here, Rebecca selected a palette of native plants chosen for their value to various pollinators as well as their beauty. To the uninitiated eye, it reads as a lush ornamental garden – a ravishingly beautiful planting scheme – but for the butterflies, it's nothing short of manna from heaven. Ecological planting that supports a broad spectrum of wildlife need not be the preserve of nature reserves or rural landscapes, it can exist in high-density urban environments too. 'Beauty is critically important; it's not a frivolity or a bonus,' Rebecca explains. 'One of my guiding principles is this old rallying cry of "Bread and Roses." It speaks to humanity's need for the necessities of a dignified life...both sustenance and beauty. I see my job, as a public servant, as bringing roses to the people.'

How wonderful it is to realize that the solutions to some of our biggest problems lie in bringing roses to the people – simply planting flowers. 'Big pictures are terrifying right now. But we can all plant a butterfly host plant. We can all support the pollinators of our neighbourhood. And those tiny steps mean so much to the plants and animals around us.' And it's something we can all do – plant a host plant, support the pollinators of our neighbourhood and fill in the gaps of a system that has evolved to survive, but is dangerously under threat. For Rebecca 'there is no place too desolate or damaged, where ecological gardening can't help', we just need to take the first step.

Observe closely and make gradual adjustments to maximize bounty

Damson Farm
Batheaston, Somerset, UK
Alison Jenkins

Permaculture, regenerative agriculture, organic growing, biodynamics – while all different, these approaches share a common goal: the desire to build a healthier relationship with the Earth and its soil. Much of the focus is on yield, nutritional value, soil health, water management and pest control. Beauty, however, is often framed as either ornamental and separate from productivity, or as secondary to ecological function. Yet when integrated thoughtfully, aesthetic value can amplify resilience and deepen our connection to the land. Our innate enjoyment of the natural world is deeply embedded in our subconscious and can be deployed to great effect when making productive gardens, because beauty itself is a yield.

Alison Jenkins, a garden designer turned edible gardener and educator, has transformed her spellbinding garden tucked away in a quiet valley outside Bath, UK, into a test bed to pioneer a new approach to gardening: regenerative gardening. A hybrid that blends elements from permaculture, organic and biodynamic practices, this approach prioritizes the health of the soil and the environment, alongside producing delicious and beautiful bounty. It's an iterative practice of observation and gentle intervention. She aims to anticipate issues before they arise and implement light-touch solutions that mimic and leverage natural processes. For example, to prevent beds from drying out and weeds germinating early in the season, Alison sows a 'duvet' of forget-me-nots. These provide insulation and act as living mulch, while offering early-season charm. Rather than a single crop per bed as in traditional kitchen gardens, Alison sows multiple crops in a bed, often intricately woven together to provide both beauty and resilience to pests. She also incorporates food forest principles, layering perennial edibles to create a system that is both productive and beautiful. Alpine strawberries and oregano make fragrant groundcovers, while fennel and rhubarb work well as a rich and textural mid-layer. By thinking holistically and continually observing and adjusting, Alison is forging a new way of growing that 'functions ecologically, provides food and looks beautiful too'.

Interest children in where food comes from at an early age

GROW
The Totteridge Academy, London, UK
GROW

Our broken relationship with food is starkly evident on the plates of millions of school children across the UK. With tight budgets, a lack of respect for food and cooking in education, and little opportunity for quality training, school lunches are often uninspiring reflections of the industrial food system – despite the best efforts of celebrity chefs and campaigners like Jamie Oliver. But in North London, a charity is pioneering a new model of farm-to-fork by hitching up a farm to a school. Few schools in capital cities around the world can claim to be directly connected to a farm, fewer still to one that supplies the school kitchen with fresh, hyper-local produce and serves as a vibrant, endlessly inspiring hands-on teaching resource across the curriculum, from biology to maths.

GROW is a two-acre farm growing fruit, vegetables and flowers run on agroecological principles, developed in partnership with The Totteridge Academy in North London.

It offers a powerful model for how farms and schools can work together to build resilient food systems, support wellbeing and strengthen community ties. The produce from the farm is sold to the school kitchen and to the local community, making a valuable contribution to the local food economy. More than just a productive growing space, GROW has become an increasingly valuable educational resource. It hosts outdoor learning programmes for children, young people and families who experience barriers to learning, healthy living and employment. These range from sustainable farming and growing to floristry and mushroom cultivation. By engaging children and young people in a holistic, land-based learning experience, GROW is equipping them with practical skills in sustainable food growing. This in turn builds resilience and curiosity, fosters community, and helps to restore a connection to nature that is all but lost in urban education.

Maximize redundant spaces – even underground

Cycloponics
Paris, Lyon and Bordeaux, France
Jean-Noël Gertz/Théo Champagnat

In the 1960s, underground car parks were a common planning requirement for new residential developments in Paris. Fast forward to today, and many of these subterranean spaces sit empty as Parisians increasingly abandon cars in favour of greener modes of transport. For Cycloponics founders Jean-Noël Gertz and Théo Champagnat, this shift presented the perfect opportunity for urban growing, but below street level. Underground, where the air temperature remains relatively steady and light levels are low, is the ideal climate for cultivating mushrooms. Shiitake, oyster and button mushrooms all thrive in the damp, dimly lit subterranean world of an underground car park. Quickly the team started experimenting with other crops, and while they found that endives and some herbs could be grown, mushrooms had the best profit margins and required the lowest input. And being in the city centre, once ready for

harvest, the mushrooms are simply loaded in crates on to the back of a bike, and delivered to local restaurants the same day. They're competitively priced for organic produce, with near-zero food miles, but as Théo told me, what suppliers are really interested in, is the exceptional quality. Having fine-tuned their model, Cycloponics now operates sites across Paris, Lyon and Bordeaux. While the car parks themselves are relatively easy to find, it can take up to two years to navigate local bureaucracy and start growing mushrooms. In addition to fungi farming, Cycloponics let their spaces to other small businesses, often start-ups looking for lower cost units for ventures ranging from bicycle repair and cold-room storage, to microgreen cultivation and craft brewing. The result is a flourishing underground economy – quite literally.

Get buy-in from the community to build scale and impact

Carioca Gardens
Rio de Janeiro, Brazil
Hortas Carioca/Julio Cesar Barros

Hortas Carioca, or Carioca Gardens, is one of the world's largest urban community garden initiatives. In 2020 alone, it produced eighty-two tonnes of fresh fruit and vegetables, most of which was donated to families hit hardest by the pandemic. The project is a direct response to a surge in Brazil's food poverty crisis, with an estimated thirty-three million Brazilians – around 15% of the population – going hungry every week. The garden is part of an ambitious project started by Julio Cesar Barros in 2006, in the heart of Manguinhos, one of Rio's largest favelas, on land once used as a rubbish dump. Managed along agroecological principles, the project is run by the municipality and locals that help tend it who in turn receive a small stipend and as much produce as they like – valuable extras when unemployment and food poverty are rife. Half of the produce is distributed to families in need, while the rest is sold at market price to supplement the incomes of those working on the project. Hortas Carioca has been such a success, both in terms of the food it is putting on the table and the sense of purpose and dignity it is restoring to the community, that there are plans to expand it further to twenty-seven acres across the district, with the goal of growing food for 50,000 local families every year. Barros and his team have proven that not only is it possible to grow food in large urban centres like Rio de Janeiro, but also that it is possible to do so at mind-boggling scale.

John Little is a gardener and designer with a penchant for waste and brownfield sites – and more recently a passionate advocate for the role of gardeners in creating healthy landscapes. At the heart of his work is a commitment to championing value in the overlooked. Much of his garden design to date highlights the undervalued potential of brownfield sites and green infrastructure, such as green roofs. Structural complexity and varied topography are the real drivers of biodiversity, often found in places we're least likely to protect – rubbish dumps, derelict land and abandoned spaces. Gardens made with low-fertility soils and substrates have the potential to be just as biodiverse than those built with nutrient-rich compost. The challenge lies in helping clients recognize these 'impoverished' landscapes for the rich ecological opportunities they truly represent.

In John's galvanizing new mission, Care Not Capital, he urges us to recognize the value in people, specifically gardeners, rather than prioritizing expensive hardscaping and design fees. This, he argues, is where real, long-term value is delivered. In public projects especially, greedy chunks of the budget often go towards construction and design firms, while ongoing care is overlooked. However, a garden or green space is not done when the contractors wrap up on the final day, the work is only just beginning. A garden matures and evolves over many years and takes the skilled eye and hand of a trained and passionate gardener to help steward that garden and maximize its potential. As this book attests, the ornamental value of the garden is only one part of the story. To deliver on the rest – biodiversity, wellbeing, resilience – you need a gardener. 'Most places don't deliver all those things unless they have someone in the know,' John says, and usually, they don't.

Care Not Capital is a community interest company that aims to train gardeners 'in everything but horticulture'. This means ecology, green infrastructure, rainwater management, biodiversity tracking and community engagement. Based at John's garden, Hilldrop in Essex, UK (see page 214), the initiative will offer means-tested training sessions designed to equip those working in public spaces with the skills to garden more creatively and dynamically. The goal is to inject public and council-run green spaces around the UK with the knowledge, insight and care that John has cultivated over his career.

As it stands, gardening budgets have been cut so drastically that the role of the gardener has been reduced to little more than litter picking, mowing, blowing and spraying. John knows this from experience. He held the gardening contract for Clapton in Hackney for twelve years, and that was all they were asked to do: 'cut grass, trim hedges, spray. No conversations with people, no understanding what people wanted, no food growing, no nothing'. As a result, the quality of public spaces has declined to fit the budget: lawns and so-called 'low-maintenance' planting – often ecologically barren – have become the norm, offering little to residents or wildlife.

However, while managing the Clapton gardens for Hackney Council, John made a point of speaking to residents (something that's made considerably harder if you're constantly wielding a mower or a leaf-blower), and soon discovered what they really wanted was some colour and a space to grow food. 'It was nothing fancy, nothing glamorous, just some 2.44 × 2.44 m (8 × 8 ft) beds to plant veg and some flowers along the railings. I also planted a grapevine for the Kurdish community to make dolmades. Cost me a tenner and it was probably the most popular thing we did.'

Undervaluing care has become normalized throughout society. It can be seen in how we treat nurses and other caring professions, as well as our elderly. But we do so at our peril. When crisis hits – as the COVID-19 pandemic so starkly demonstrated – we soon realize what vital roles these overlooked professions deliver. Right now, we're in the midst of other crises – environmental, social and more besides. Gardens could play a powerful role in helping to mitigate the worst effects, but only if we begin to truly value gardeners and the breadth of their skills. With John flying the flag, it feels likely that we might finally start to do just that.

Reinvent the productive garden for office life

Pasona Urban Farm
Tokyo, Japan
Kono Designs

The urban-rural divide is a form of political and cultural polarization. Divergent views at each end of the spectrum can result in a fundamental lack of empathy and understanding about how others live. In increasingly urban societies, this sense of disconnection from rural life, including agriculture and the fundamentals of where food comes from, is a gap that's hard to bridge. When Japanese recruitment firm Pasona decided to refurbish its Tokyo headquarters, it seized the opportunity to address this gap. Beyond the obvious rooftop garden, Pasona has integrated urban farming facilities throughout the building, resulting in a 'farm' that houses over 200 species of plants, fruits and vegetables. Employees are actively encouraged to tend and harvest the produce. Tomato vines are suspended above

conference tables, fruit trees act as living partitions between meeting spaces and bean sprouts are grown under benches. In an atrium, a rice paddy fills the raised beds – harvested each season by employees.

All produce grown at the offices is prepared and served on site, in a hyper-local farm-to-table café, closing the loop between growing and eating. Pasona's commitment to reconnecting its staff with growing food has meant it has had to sacrifice office space to plant beds, but the compromise has been well worth it, providing an improved workspace for its employees and a small but significant effort to reconnect city-dwellers with the story of their food.

Revive heritage crops to restore food and financial security

Africa Kaki Community Garden
Mutitu, Kirinyaga County, Kenya
Slow Food International

Heritage varieties and traditional ways of farming that are kinder to the planet and foster more stable food systems are being eroded by the dominance of cash-crops in many rural economies across the Global South. Where farmers once grew food to eat and sold the surplus, they are now growing solely for export. The result? Many barely make sufficient profit to buy food. In Uganda (and dozens of other countries across Africa), Slow Food is trying to challenge this through its 'Food Gardens in Africa Project', which empowers farmers to grow heritage crops on a more domestic scale that bolsters local food security and can be eaten and sold at the local market, instead of global commodities like sugarcane. In these communities, it's not uncommon for farmers to sign contracts with global agriculture companies with just a thumb print. These agreements lock them into extractive practices like monocropping, which degrade the land and leave farmers out of pocket. Instead, Slow Food encourages farmers to grow native crops for the local economy, which require lower inputs and increase biodiversity. Traditional vegetable varieties such as *nduma*, a type of taro root, are at risk of extinction due to global homogenization, along with the Indigenous farming methods used to cultivate them. By re-establishing these crops and techniques, the project has revived the fortunes of a vast network of farmers from villages and regions across the continent. These farmers are sharing invaluable local knowledge on everything from pest control to irrigation – methods that might have otherwise been lost to the pressures of 'progress'.

Reduce noise pollution, purify the air and filter sunlight with planting

Urban Farm
Ho Chi Minh City, Vietnam
Vo Trong Nghia (VTN) Architects

Ho Chi Minh City, one of the fastest-growing cities in Southeast Asia, has transformed from dense tropical wetlands along the banks of the Mekong River into a sprawling metropolis in just a generation. The speed of change has had predictable consequences – flooding, pollution, the heat-island effect and an increasingly grey landscape, which are all now features of Ho Chi Minh City life. For a nation deeply connected to food, these challenges are both practical and emotional, particularly as floods and salinization threaten food supplies. This is a problem that Vo Trong Nghia (VTN) Architects sought to overcome with its Urban Farming Office.

Vo Trong Nghia, a Vietnamese architectural practice, has made connecting city residents to nature its company's *raison d'être*, adopting a garden-first approach to much of their design. For their office in Thu Duc district, they took this one step further, smothering the building not just in plants, but edible ones, transforming it into a vertical farm. The design boasts a 190% green-to-grey ratio for the building, which produces one tonne of harvest in a space that would historically have yielded nothing. Beyond providing fresh, locally grown organic fruit and vegetables to appreciative staff, this density of planting also greatly reduces the need for other inputs, filtering direct sunlight, reducing noise and purifying the air. An in-house irrigation system that reuses stormwater and the natural cooling from evaporation creates a space that truly embodies the meaning of a healthy work–life balance.

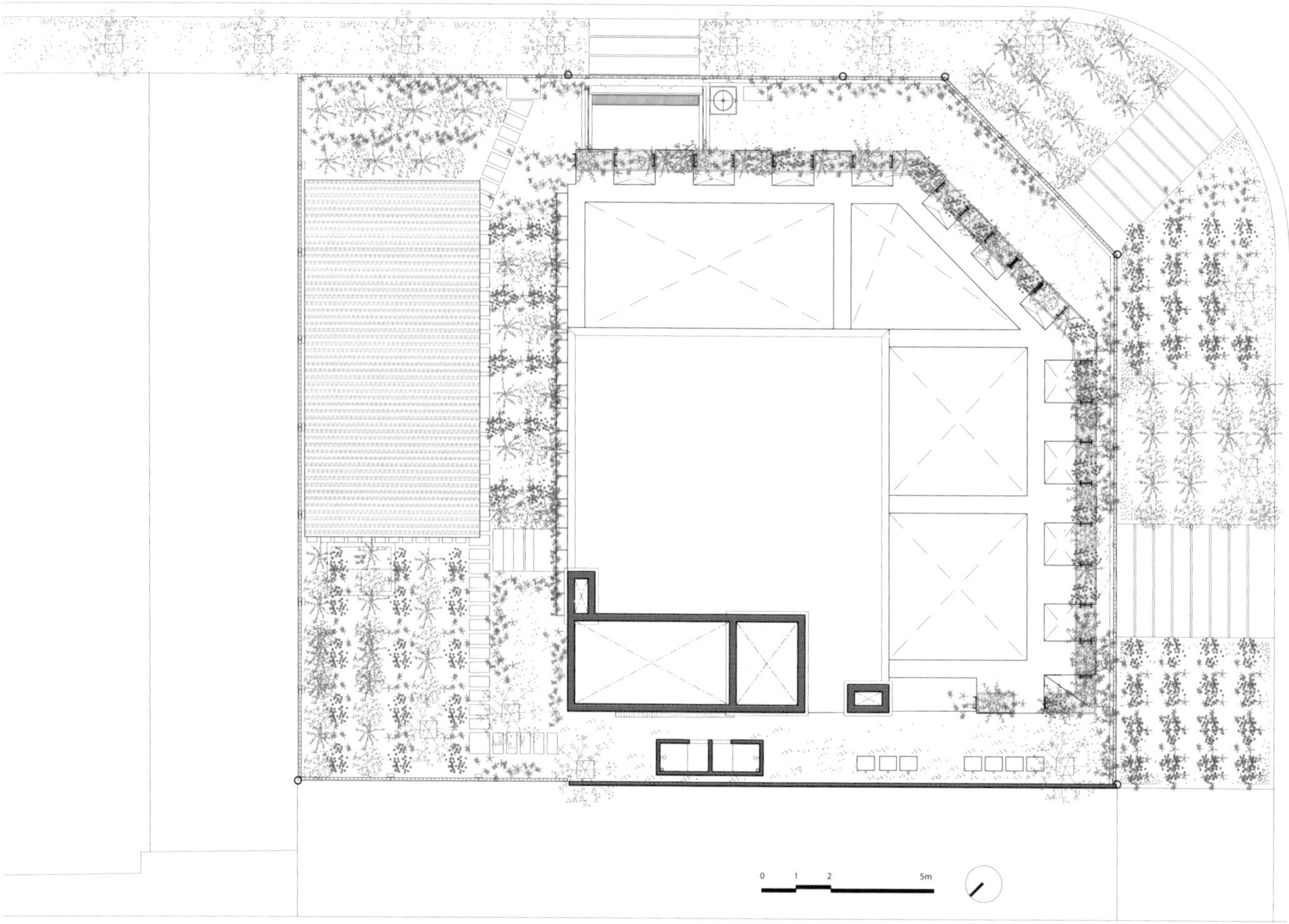

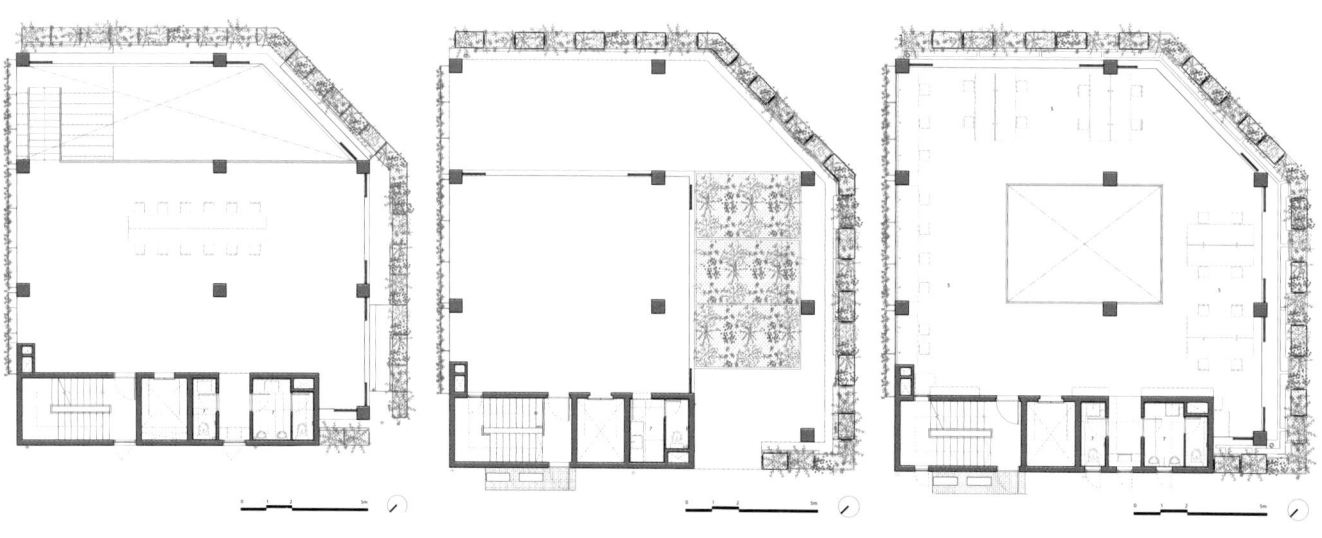

Enrich barren land with permaculture

Changpas Mountain Garden
Ladakh, Kashmir
Dr Jigmet Yangchan

For permaculture specialist Dr Jigmet Yangchan, the arid mountain plains of Ladakh in Kashmir presented a particularly challenging brief. This region is barren and wild, with a temperature range of -30 to +30 °C (-86 to +86 °F) throughout the year. It receives almost no rainfall, has thin, nutrient-deficient soils, little to no infrastructure and is situated over 5,000 m above sea level. As a result, the communities that live in this inhospitable region are largely nomadic, relying on cattle for both sustenance and livelihood. Malnutrition is widespread, especially in children, due to the scarcity of vegetables in their diets. Despite these challenges, Jigmet was undeterred. A passionate advocate and skilled practitioner of permaculture, she created a three-year plan to establish a vegetable garden and give villagers better food and financial security. She started with a permaculture fundamental: vermiculture (worm composting). The extreme weather and altitude meant that the cycle to break down waste into usable compost took up to five months, compared to the usual forty-five days in warmer climates.

Next, she focused on improving the microbial activity in the barren soil. Jigmet developed a natural fertilizer using cow dung, cow urine, chickpea flour, jaggery (a raw sugar), soil and water to nourish the earth. Water was another challenge. Jigmet rigged up a system to extract groundwater using the plentiful solar energy, generating just enough to have a low-tech irrigation system for the productive beds.

All this effort needed protection, yet natural materials such as bark for mulch were unavailable in the high desert plains, so polythene was used to keep the precious new nutrients and moisture content in the soil. Three years after embarking on this epic undertaking, the gardens now boast crops of aubergines, lentils, okra, garlic, cauliflowers, peppers, tomatoes and even watermelons. The next task is teaching nomadic residents, unfamiliar with such techniques, how to replicate this; how to cultivate the land and grow their own crops. Jigmet says her proudest moment during the project was receiving the first crop of garlic from the village – a gift traditionally reserved for God – an apt tribute for someone who has worked true miracles.

HEAL

Nature's power to heal is so deeply understood that it seems almost strange that science is only now catching up with what we have instinctively always known. Yet, in recent history, our previously unbroken bond with nature was severed in pursuit of a new way of living. In our high-density urban model, the once-intuitive rhythms of the natural world have been pushed to the margins, and often erased entirely. This abrupt shift has undone thousands of years of harmonious symbiosis, the consequences of which we're only just beginning to unravel.

For the billions of us living in urban environments, nature is no longer an integral part of our day-to-day lives, but something we must actively seek out. Access to green space is on the decline - eroded by austerity, privatization and poorly considered development, leaving public spaces barren and depriving those who need them most. Even those with the luxury of private green spaces have often embraced the convenience of 'low-maintenance' solutions, trading nature-rich spaces for AstroTurf and concrete, rather than pottering in a garden at the end of a long working week.

It's no coincidence that our growing alienation from nature has paralleled the rise of chronic health conditions, placing an immense burden on global health systems. Stress, high blood pressure, increased allergies, weakened immunity and poor mental health have become weary hallmarks of 21st-century life. Robin Wall Kimmerer, author of the best-selling *Braiding Sweetgrass: Indigenous Wisdom, Scientific Knowledge and the Teachings of Plants*, talks of 'species loneliness' - a profound, universal sadness born from our estrangement from the natural world, leaving many of us feeling lonely and isolated. This rupture doesn't just affect our minds; it takes a physical toll too. Studies consistently show a positive correlation between access to green space and improved heart health, lower cholesterol, reduced rates of diabetes and obesity.

However, gardens and green spaces are increasingly being recognized as a cure to myriad modern maladies, from PTSD and postnatal depression to loneliness and infertility, and rightly so. Hundreds of thousands of years of co-evolution have cast a deep evolutionary shadow on both our collective consciousness and our biology. Our need for nature is profound and undeniable, woven into the very fabric of our existence. This has been well documented across civilizations and cultures around the world, long before the first gardens were cultivated.

It's only in the last 100 of our 300,000-year human history that we haven't lived in close connection with the land. Our need to be closely aligned with nature is hard-wired into our very DNA. In *Biophilia: The human bond with other species*, American biologist Edward O. Wilson argued that our affinity for nature has a genetic basis - a biological necessity ingrained in us through millennia of co-evolution. In this context, it should come as no surprise that severing our connection to the natural world has profound developmental consequences, both for individuals and for our species as a whole.

In landscape design, we're taught prospect and refuge theory. This is the idea that different spatial configurations can engender distinct emotional responses. We derive feelings of safety and pleasure in spaces that offer both views (prospect) and a sense of enclosure (refuge). Anyone who has experienced the comfort of a tree canopy, or the security of standing on a hilltop, will recognize these fundamentals at play here. At its most basic, our aesthetic appreciation of landscapes is rooted in their suitability for survival. In our ancestral environments, the most favourable landscapes combined open grasslands for hunting and grazing, dotted with trees for shelter and protection. These same landscapes, optimal for survival, remain the ones we find most aesthetically pleasing - an idea woven deep into our collective unconscious.

Given our long and happy relationship with nature, it comes as no surprise that being absorbed in an idealized natural setting is central to many garden traditions across both the ancient and modern world. Persian pleasure gardens, Islamic paradise gardens, Chinese courtyard gardens and Japanese rock gardens all foster a deep sense of natural immersion that predates our contemporary fascination with gardens. The idea that gardens are a place of contemplative reflection and intellectual stimulation first found footing in Roman courtyards, where one could study life sciences and botany, while marvelling at the gentle patterns and rhythms of nature. Later, monasteries would typically include enclosed gardens (*hortus conclusus*) designed for meditation and recuperation, reinforcing the understanding that fresh air and green spaces profoundly influence human physiology and psychology.

In many Indigenous cultures, where a land-based approach to life persists, the distinction between 'man' and 'nature' simply does not exist, for we *are* nature. This is reflected in many Indigenous languages, which lack words to express this separation or instead animate the natural world with personal pronouns and mythic narratives. Echoes of this innate understanding of nature can be seen in children who pay no heed to modern culture's sterile objectification of the outdoors. They instinctively anthropomorphize plants and animals in play, seek solace in the earth and lie on the ground to calm themselves when overwhelmed. That we must now actively look for opportunities to commune with nature would feel as alien to our ancestors as the notion of hunting and gathering does to us.

Today, gardens are reclaiming their rightful place in our therapeutic toolbox, drawing on a tradition first formalized in the Middle Ages. Historically, hospital gardens provided not only vegetables and medicinal plants but also spaces for quiet contemplation and recuperation. However, in modern settings, they have fallen out of favour, sacrificed to the demands of clinical efficiency and advances in medecine. Yet, in our increasingly sick world, their utility is finally being validated by modern science. Healing gardens are now being built as integral therapeutic resources in hospitals, hospices and clinics around the world. Study after study confirms that access to green space aids recovery - in fact you need only a view of a green space, instead of say a car park, to enjoy better health outcomes.

And just as our minds have evolved to find calm beneath canopies, our bodies have adapted to coexist with the natural world too. The rise in obesity, stress and high blood pressure, and the lowering of immunity, point to a global malaise, one that gardens have the potential to help alleviate. New avenues in research are empirically corroborating the healing powers of natural environments. For example, stress responses can be measured (or notably reduced) depending on our surroundings. This discovery has fuelled the global adoption of forest bathing, or *shinrin-yoku*, beyond its origins in Japan. Forests help regulate our parasympathetic nervous system (the body's 'rest and recover' mechanism) while also reducing cortisol and adrenaline levels, blood pressure and heart rate. Additionally, trees release phytoncides, chemical compounds that protect them from pests and disease, but also have powerful effects on human health. Sleeping in a room infused with these compounds has been shown to boost the production of natural killer cells, which help the body detect and fight early signs of cancer. Similarly,

direct contact with soil - something increasingly absent from modern life - can help replenish beneficial microbes and restore gut biodiversity, both of which are essential for intestinal and overall health. Re-establishing our relationship with nature is the key to unlocking the wealth of benefits gardens and green spaces offer for our wellbeing. The true magic lies in this relationship, which you might call the reciprocal dance between nature and man. The awe-inspiring wonder of a glade or meadow is not incidental; it is a mechanism designed to capture our attention, evoke reverence and inspire stewardship. When we feel invested in nature, we are more likely to protect it. Yet this system of mutual benefit that evolved to keep us both well is woefully out of balance. By prioritizing and investing in the great outdoors, we can restore nature's ability to heal us in the many ways it always has always done. And in doing so, we may ultimately find ourselves healing nature in return.

A sculpture by Sofía Táboas in The Botanic Garden, →
Culiacán, Mexico (pp.178-81).

Sow plants with healing properties to bolster modern healthcare

Trapa Trapa Forest
Santiago, Chile
Symbiótica/SUGi

Chile's largest native ethnic group, the Mapuche, who live predominantly in the Temuco area of southern Chile, have long relied on a wide variety of herbal remedies to treat ailments from arthritis and acne to digestive issues and low libido. In the grounds of the Sótero del Río Hospital, SUGi forest maker Symbiótica drew on this deep well of Indigenous knowledge to imbue the garden with cultural and medicinal heritage.

The Trapa Trapa Forest features a variety of native species, each with traditional healing properties. *Aristotelia chilensis* (maqui) is valued for its anti-inflammatory benefits, *Buddleja globosa* (matico) leaves are used to cleanse wounds and treat skin conditions, *Quillaja saponaria* (quillay) aids respiratory problems, and *Peumus boldus* (boldo) is believed to stimulate bile production and support digestion. Nestled beside a bustling road, this immersive forest garden offers a sanctuary from noise and pollution, and a place to reconnect with ancient wisdom and the healing power of nature. The presence of local plants has also brought diverse wildlife to the garden, including thrushes, blackbirds, doves and tufted tits, adding their song to the soundscape. The garden is also a fitting backdrop for the hospital's 'Sonrisólogos' team, Su and Carola, who are professional laughter therapists. The Trapa Trapa Forest has become a source of green respite that seamlessly weaves ancient wisdom, nature and modern healthcare together, fostering healing and a deeper understanding of the connection between people and the planet. As Carola says, 'a hospital does not have to be a sad place. Despite the difficulties, we are there to sow joy and hope.'

Seek calm in the canopy of trees and watch stress levels drop

Forest Bathing
Tokyo, Japan
Forest Therapy Society

If you have ever lain on your back and looked up at a canopy of trees, you may be familiar with the deep sense of calm that floods your nervous system. This is a response embedded in our collective unconscious. This universal phenomenon, known as forest bathing, or *shinrin-yoku*, was formally recognized by the Japanese Ministry of Agriculture, Forestry, and Fisheries in 1982. It was introduced as part of a national health initiative as an antidote to the stresses of urbanization and Japan's increasingly high-pressure work culture.

Since then, Dr Qing Li, a leading immunologist and expert in forest medicine, has rigorously studied the practice, confirming its profound benefits. Scientific research now shows that forest bathing can reduce stress, lower blood pressure, improve immunity, boost the production of anti-cancer proteins, improve mood disorders, and even enhance sleep quality and overall wellbeing.

The benefits of spending time in forests are so well recognized in Japan that forest bathing is routinely prescribed by doctors and more than seventy designated 'healing forests' now exist across the country. The Forest Therapy Society has established a strict set of standards to certify (and protect) these forests for *shinrin-yoku* and continues to study their impact on human health and wellbeing. Dr Qing Li notes that it is no surprise that forest bathing became so popular in Japan, as both Shinto and Buddhist traditions regard forests as the realm of the divine. Moreover, silviculture – the careful cultivation and management of trees – has long been embedded in Japanese culture. For centuries, groves of *sugi* (Japanese cedar) and *hinoki* (cypress) have been nurtured and tended to both for ceremonial purposes and for use in vernacular architecture.

Yet the healing power of nature is not limited to Japan. Even an hour spent mindfully walking in a city park, just observing closely the patterns and rhythms of nature, can have a transformative effect on your state of mind and health. Even more reason to ensure that everyone has access to the healing benefits of the wild and that the provision of green space is seen as critical to public health.

Use biomimicry to recreate evocative soundscapes

Harry Johnson Memorial Garden
Melbourne, Australia
Phillip Johnson Landscapes

When landscape designer Phillip Johnson was approached by his client Maria, who had recently been widowed, to create a garden in memory of her husband in her small suburban backyard in Melbourne, Australia, he jumped at the opportunity. Maria had a deep love of water, not just for its soothing, healing qualities, but also for the happy memories it evoked. She and her late husband, Harry, had spent years camping near a creek in the Grampians National Park in Western Victoria, and she longed to bring a piece of that experience into her home.

With just 15 m² (162 ft²) to play with, Phillip set out to recreate this memory of the creek for Maria – the sights, the sounds, the smell, and the feeling of being creek-side – but within an urban setting. To do this authentically, he turned to biomimicry: the practice of learning from and mimicking nature's systems to solve human design challenges. In order to create a truly authentic soundscape, Phillip and his team meticulously studied every aspect of the creek's natural design and evolution. How did the placement of rocks influence the speed of water passing through the creek? What size were the stones in the shallows, and how did they affect the sound of water running over them? How did these elements attract specific insects and birds, contributing to the auditory landscape? Thinking at this level of detail has an effect on the types of insect and animal drawn to the garden, which in turn would affect the sound and feeling of the garden. Through careful observation and replication of these natural dynamics, Phillip and his team slowly crafted a miniature version of the creek-side experience that not only looked and sounded like the original, but also functioned like it too. By mimicking strategies that have evolved in nature, they created a garden that was both deeply personal and ecologically connected. The result was a space that brought Maria peace and nostalgia, while also connecting a small patch of suburbia to a much broader ecological context within the rhythm and harmony of the wild.

Look to landscapes that inspire awe and wonder for faster healing

Healing Garden
Samaritan Lebanon Community Hospital, Oregon, USA
Kurisu International

The Healing Garden at Samaritan Lebanon Community Hospital transformed a small rural hospital into a nationally recognized, award-winning model of progressive healthcare. Patients can receive treatment with views of the impressively planted landscape or fully immerse themselves within it. Beyond the hospital, the garden kickstarted a ripple effect throughout the otherwise unremarkable and underfunded town. The benefits of the garden were so evident and far-reaching that Kurisu was soon commissioned to design additional gardens for the broader community to enjoy, initiating a transformation of the entire area. 'The impact of the Healing Garden on our patients and on our physicians and staff has been nothing short of extraordinary. From morale and pride to patient care, to a spirit of healing and recovery, it profoundly affects us every day,' enthuses the hospital's CEO, Becky Pape.

Led by first-generation Japanese immigrant Hoichi Kurisu, the landscape firm creates gardens grounded in the ancient philosophies and techniques of Japanese garden design. Its work fosters a deep reconnection between people and nature, aligning with the larger, timeless cycles of change and regeneration. 'Japanese gardens evolved for one purpose: to make you more present,' explains Michiko Kurisu, Hoichi's daughter.

Japanese garden design – arguably one of Japan's most renowned exports – integrates natural elements such as water and planting in careful balance, creating an atmosphere of calm and restoration. While these principles are ancient, modern science substantiates the link between certain natural environments and wellbeing. Rachel and Stephen Kaplan's Attention Restoration Theory (ART) talks about the restorative effects of 'effortless attention' in places that evoke awe and wonder, and allow you to feel connected with nature and removed from everyday life. Japanese gardens particularly excel at this, setting the stage for personal transformation to happen. As Michiko puts it so eloquently, 'healing starts when you have a receptive mind'.

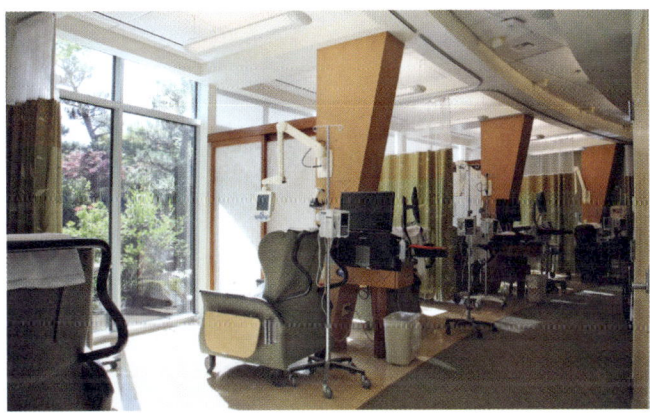

Think carefully about the needs of the people using a garden

Horatio's Garden
Stanmore, UK
Tom Stuart-Smith, and other designers at various locations nationwide

Life can change in an instant. For those coming to terms with the life-altering reality of a spinal injury, gardens provide a vital refuge, offering a space for reflection away from the clinical formality of a hospital ward. Horatio's Garden is a UK charity established in honour of Horatio Chapple, a schoolboy with aspirations of becoming a doctor, who tragically lost his life in 2011. During his time volunteering at the Duke of Cornwall Spinal Treatment Centre, Horatio recognized a need for outdoor spaces where patients with spinal injuries and their loved ones could spend time. Following his untimely death, an outpouring of love and goodwill led to the creation of the first Horatio's Garden site, specifically designed to support those adjusting to life with a spinal injury. Thirteen years later, the charity has flourished, now nurturing nine gardens across the UK with more to come, collectively supporting the wellbeing of thousands of patients, families and NHS staff.

Privacy and reflection are at the heart of these gardens, providing the space for patients and families to process life-changing news, share time together during the long months of rehabilitation, and for staff to unwind and relax during a busy working day. Thoughtful ergonomic design ensures accessibility. Wide, smooth paths accommodate wheelchairs and hospital beds, while raised planting beds are positioned at an optimal height so patients can interact with plants and enjoy the sensory benefits of nature. As rehabilitation begins, often a long and at times demoralizing process, the gardens offer valuable opportunities to regain fine motor skills, whether through planting seeds or deadheading flowers. They're also an essential link to the outside world in the first stages of rehabilitation, helping patients reconnect with daily life. Growing your own vegetables, picking flowers for your bedside, and simply being surrounded by nature can be powerful reminders of normalcy and independence.

Victoria Holton, a Trustee of Horatio's Garden who spent nineteen months in hospital following a spinal injury, describes their impact: 'These extraordinary, beautiful and vibrant spaces have revolutionized people's experience during their long hospital stays and are critical to the incredibly challenging process of coming to terms with a spinal injury.'

Nigel Dunnett Planting Designer and Professor of Planting Design and Urban Horticulture at the University of Sheffield

Nigel Dunnett is one of the most respected voices in British planting design, with an influence that extends far beyond the UK. Whether consciously or not, many of the projects featured in this book owe something to his vision. Over the past two decades, he has been the creative force behind some of the most celebrated landscape projects, including the Barbican (see page 68), the Tower of London Superbloom, Sheffield's 'Grey to Green' initiative, and many more. The ripple effect of his work has transformed the way we think about urban landscapes, bringing dynamic, nature-led planting into cities and setting a new standard for what these spaces can – and should – deliver. While his designs are celebrated for their ecological integrity and their ability to meet the functional demands of urban planning, his true muse is wonder: the desire to inspire awe through beautiful, enriching landscapes.

Nigel has been gardening since he was a child. As a boy, he had a small plot of his own to tend, growing lettuces and radishes, picking up tips from the BBC's *Gardeners' World* and absorbing the enthusiastic, if somewhat traditional, gardening practices of 1970s Britain. But it was a formative experience in a wood in his early teens that pointed him on his way, radically changing the way he thought about gardens, a eureka moment that remains the bedrock of his thinking today.

While exploring the countryside where he grew up, he came across a bluebell wood in spring. 'I got these feelings of wonder and awe and just rightness, being in the middle of a fantastically beautiful meadow or wonderful woodland. I had never had that feeling in the garden, so I started to think, why might that be?' Back in his garden he began to experiment, mixing and blending plants in random and organic patterns, rather than blocking them out in rigid formations as was the received wisdom at the time. The mixes were imitations of the bluebell wood – swathes and drifts, naturalistic groupings that we are now very familiar with, that at the time were unusual. His goal was 'purely instinctive' – to evoke the same emotion he felt in the bluebell wood and it remains his inspiration today.

For Nigel, this distinctly artistic approach to creating gardens, one where aesthetics and emotion are primary drivers, is key: 'it has to work for people, regardless of how ecologically sound it is'. This is not an opinion shared by everyone. In a climate emergency, there are people who believe that aesthetics should be secondary – what matters is that landscapes and gardens deliver ecological benefit, and what the landscape looks like is irrelevant. But for Nigel this somewhat joyless and puritanical view misses the point entirely. These spaces are an opportunity to provoke an emotional response. 'It's about how they make you feel...and what I try and do with my work is

provoke an extremely positive emotional response in people.' Human engagement is as important as ecological functioning, particularly in the urban context, where environments are designed primarily for people. 'If we can't engage people and get them to really love it and want more of it, then it's never going to be mainstream. It has to have that artistic aesthetic, that communion.' Much like art, 'if it's really working, it should be almost instinctive to understand it'.

Intuition is an increasingly rare commodity in modern life. With libraries of information (in varying shades of veracity) at our fingertips, it's all too easy to ask Google or AI rather than trust our gut instinct. This applies both to how we garden our own gardens, and how we train people to garden public gardens. At the Barbican, for example, a dynamic scheme of designed plant communities, Nigel believes that 'you need gardeners who are able to make their own decisions, do things on site without a supervisor having told them what to do. The most important thing is this empowerment of gardeners and for them to feel ownership over what they're doing'.

Similarly, in our own gardens, we labour under the idea that it's all so much more complex than it is. Latin names and intimidating language stand in our way, and preconceived notions of control over nature lock us into joyless relationships with our gardens. We battle against what a place already is, imposing our idea of what should grow where, and how it should look, a folly that even Nigel is not immune to. 'Gardening, traditionally, is a battle against what a place wants to be,' he says, and for the first few years in his garden in Sheffield, this is how Nigel worked, removing plants that weren't 'meant' to be there to maintain the vision he had in his head. 'But I've changed my whole attitude to it being more like a conversation with nature. What would the garden be if I stepped back a little bit?' It stops being a battle and becomes a dialogue. The process of garden-making becomes more enjoyable and the garden turns into what it wants to be.

Despite the depressing context, climate change presents an amazing opportunity to create transformative gardens and landscapes that inspire human engagement and restore our respect and love for the natural world. These could be high-profile projects such as London's Queen Elizabeth II Memorial Garden for which Nigel is the ecology consultant, or a simple log pile in your own garden. 'You can develop as much fascination in a square metre [as in a larger space]; there are so many lessons and bigger picture things just within that'. Whatever the scale, it's through this balance of both the mind of the artist and the ecologist, that Nigel is able to unlock the true potential of gardens for both people and planet.

Build identity and pride with world-class art and design

The Botanic Garden
Tatiana Bilbao Estudio, Culiacán, Mexico
Tatiana Bilbao, Augustin Coppel and Patrick Charpenal

Gardens can be a tool to heal our minds and bodies, and this is the case not just for individuals, but for entire communities. In Culiacán, a city in northwestern Mexico known for its banda music and rich Sinaloan culture, violence has long overshadowed everyday life. For years it has been the battleground on which Sinaloa Cartel play out their drug wars. Infamously, it was the stage for the Battle of Culiacán, where authorities attempted – and failed – to arrest the son of cartel kingpin El Chapo. Yet while the violence continues, the residents, known as *culichis*, are finding identity in a different narrative for their city, namely a world-class botanical garden.

Over the last twenty years, the gardens have become a catalyst for significant positive change and investment. Local businessman Augustin Coppel, alongside Mexican architect Tatiana Bilbao and curator Patrick Charpenal, has led a multidisciplinary effort to transform the public space into a park that residents can be proud of, reshaping the narrative of Culiacán. Enhancing the already spectacular gardens, the team has cultivated a world-class collection of bamboos and palms. Additionally, Charpenal and Coppel together have acquired, commissioned and curated a contemporary art collection that holds its own on a global stage, featuring works by Richard Long, Dan Graham, Gabriel Orozco, Olafur Eliasson and James Turrell.

This has transformed how residents feel about their city – it has instilled a sense of hope against the bloody backdrop of violence and provided a much-needed refuge and oasis in the urban landscape. Perhaps the most powerful symbol of the garden's success in forging a new identity for this damaged city is James Turrell's installation, which is now emblazoned on Mexican Airways promotional material. The garden has not just become an emblem of local pride, but of national identity.

Create the space for children to forge a relationship with nature

Serge Hill Project for Gardening, Creativity and Health
Bedmond, Hertfordshire, UK
Sue and Tom Stuart-Smith

The link between gardens and mental wellbeing is now well established, thanks in large part to psychotherapists like Sue Stuart-Smith and her book *The Well Gardened Mind* (see page 36). However, awareness alone isn't enough. The real challenge is access. Many people can't get outdoors into nature, and often they are those with the greatest need. At Serge Hill, Sue Stuart-Smith has set up a Community Interest Company (CIC) dedicated to providing that access. The initiative welcomes children from the local primary school and adults with learning disabilities from a local charity, with future plans to incorporate social prescribing. The heart of the project is the Plant Library, created in collaboration with her husband, renowned landscape designer Tom Stuart-Smith. Originally conceived as a resource for landscape designers, gardeners and hobbyists, it now also serves as a sanctuary for visitors to the Serge Hill Project.

While not all therapeutic gardens are fortunate enough to be designed by one of the world's leading landscape architects, their true value lies not in design, but in the freedom they offer for exploration and immersion. Sue notes that children quickly lose themselves in the garden, happily exploring the maze of planting and absorbed in the sensory experience. The activities Sue and her team devise for children are beautifully simple. After spending some time in the garden, each child selects a favourite flower, brings it to the Apple House (a structure designed and built by Sue's son Ben), and draws their chosen bloom.

This is a simple activity anyone can replicate at home, but what is crucial, Sue explains, 'is to plant that experience, so it's in their memories. If they've had a good experience in the garden and in the natural world, they might return to it'. Nurturing a connection with nature in childhood gives children the best chance of reaping rewards in later life. It's a formative seed, one that may not germinate for years to come, but when it does, it might just grow into an oak.

HEAL

Leverage biophilic principles and watch your health improve

Khoo Teck Puat Hospital
Yishun, Singapore
CPG Consultants/RMJM Architecture

The brief for this hospital's design, set by its former CEO, was simple yet ambitious: she wanted her blood pressure to lower upon entering the hospital grounds. Achieving this in an environment typically associated with high-pressure, life-or-death situations was a tall order, but the resulting design manages to not just achieve this, but completely reinvent what a hospital could be.

Biophilic principles have been woven into every stage of the design process. The building's V-shaped structure was carefully planned and designed to capture and channel prevailing north and east winds, reducing the need for air conditioning by 60% – a remarkable feat for a hospital in the tropics. Greenery envelops the building, with dense, forest-like planting extending across all available horizontal and vertical planes, achieving a green ratio nearly four times the hospital's footprint.

Balconies provide further opportunities for planting, filled with scented plants to bring the sensory benefits of nature directly into patients' rooms, while the hospital grounds resemble a lush park. A thriving farm grows over 150 species of fruits and vegetables, tended to and managed by volunteers from a nearby neighbourhood and supplying fresh produce to the hospital's organic kitchen. Additionally, a dementia garden on level four caters for the specific needs of Alzheimer's patients, offering a therapeutic space for rest and recovery.

Adored by staff and visitors alike, Khoo Teck Puat Hospital attracts a high number of patient visitors and unsurprisingly consistently outperforms all other hospitals in Singapore in the Ministry of Health's annual satisfaction survey. This project is a glowing example of the power of biophilic design and how to integrate it effectively in a modern healthcare setting.

Yun Hye Hwang Associate Professor of Landscape Architecture at the University of Singapore

One of the great challenges in landscape design today is how to bring the benefits of gardens – in particular, the highly potent, dynamic wild variety – to the confines of a city. Cities, by definition, are our most nature-depleted environments, yet they are also the most densely populated. They are the places the restorative power of the wild is most needed, and paradoxically, the places least compatible with it. Yun Hye Hwang, Associate Professor of Landscape Architecture at the University of Singapore, has dedicated much of her career to finding design solutions to this conundrum. Her work explores how the urban, the wild and the tame can coexist, and the multifunctional role of urban green spaces in high-density cities.

A gleaming paean to modernity like Singapore might seem like an unlikely place to push the boundaries of urban rewilding. And it's true that historically, there have been concerns about straying too far from a manicured aesthetic to one that embraces ecological richness and wildness. 'Public agencies may feel pressured by complaints about mosquitoes breeding or unwanted animals like snakes hiding in tall grass. Safety concerns also arise, such as tall grass posing fire risks during dry weather or obstructing traffic views,' Yun Hye explains. The fear that exists about the wild – the imagined threats, the concern about 'mess' and disease – is remarkably consistent, from Singapore to Santiago. Yun Hye's work focuses on the design strategies that can be deployed to quell these fears without compromising the ecological benefits of less-managed urban green spaces.

The first of these strategies is the use of 'cues to care', a term that was coined by landscape architect Joan Nassauer in 1995 to describe design elements that signal human care and maintenance. The idea is that, by incorporating just enough of these visual cues, the landscape can still be read as cared for, even if much of it is left loose, wild, or less intensively managed. This might include a mown border framing a wilder, unmown centre, crisp boundary edging, or a neatly pruned tree. The goal is to communicate intentionality in the midst of natural abundance. Getting this balance right is 'essential' for gaining public support for urban greening, says Yun Hye. We need our green spaces to feel loved and cared for in order for people to feel comfortable, safe and welcome within them.

Another approach focuses on the ways in which urban green spaces can strengthen the links between residents and wildlife. With the right design strategies in place, cities can become places that don't just tolerate wildlife and the 'more-than-human' but actively support it. Traditionally, human-wildlife interactions have been largely absent from planning and design, which have typically taken an anthropocentric approach, relegating wildlife to designated nature reserves. However, in Singapore, this ecological connectivity is embedded throughout the city's urban fabric. For example, wildlife corridors (see Glossary) are created through visibly connected tree canopies, tree-top overpasses for birds and arboreal fauna, and even overhead bridges above highways, two of which in Singapore are designed exclusively for wildlife. When habitats are designed and supported by appropriate safeguards and public education, encounters between people and wildlife become more frequent and accepted. This helps to normalize these interactions and reframe wildlife as an integral part of our shared environment, rather than something separate or other.

It's easy to see Singapore as an exception. It's a tropical city with a government that has the resources and wherewithal to support this style of urban greening. But Yun Hye argues that unmanaged urban green spaces 'hold significant potential' as alternative green infrastructure, particularly in underprivileged communities across the Global South. We should be protecting and retrofitting existing unmanaged green spaces rather than removing them during development. 'These spaces should be treated as necessities,' she insists. They deliver vital ecosystem services, livelihood opportunities and pollution mitigation, alongside their ecological potential.

For Yun Hye, urban novel ecosystems (human-shaped habitats that contain species that have not historically occurred) are 'transformative'. They restore biodiversity and create vibrant spaces that celebrate regional identity. Her work reimagines urban tropical landscapes as biodiverse, dynamic and ecologically integrated systems. In an era of rapid urbanization and climate change, the need to transition from manicured urban landscapes to rewilded ones is more urgent than ever. But, as she demonstrates, with the right design strategies in place, it is entirely possible to harmonize human and ecological needs.

Integrate sensory elements to offer respite during challenging times

Children's Hospice Gardens
Various locations, UK
Greenfingers Charity

For children with life-limiting illnesses and their families, time spent together is painfully precious, making the quality of that time vital. Hospice gardens provide space for play, exploration, therapy, reflection and relaxation. Often they're simply somewhere to spend time together. Greenfingers Charity has created over seventy children's hospice gardens across the UK, benefiting thousands of children, their families and carers.

These are sensory gardens, designed to engage all five senses, with aromatic plants to smell, edibles to taste, grasses that swoosh and rattle, and a variety of textures to run your hands through and lay your eyes on. At Little Harbour Children's Hospice in St Austell, UK, designer Darren Hawkes includes a shelter so that children and families can be outside irrespective of the often-temperamental Cornish weather. At

Claire House Children's Hospice, Carolyn Willitts has created a sensory feast. 'We wanted to inject colour, humour, curiosity and whimsy along the way, inspiring stories and interactive play,' she says. A rainbow meadow of vibrant planting attracts plumes of pollinators, a 'Creation Station' invites children to get their hands dirty and play with soil and plants, and a quiet zone offers space for calm and contemplation.

Accessibility is central to these gardens, ensuring wheelchair users can navigate freely and experience immersive planting at child-friendly heights. While the physical benefits of time spent in gardens are well known, for families living with life-threatening or life-limiting illnesses, these spaces are vital opportunities to create meaningful memories away from the clinical setting of the bedside.

Heal from trauma in thoughtful woodland environments

Nordic Therapy Garden
Kyiv, Ukraine
Mikael Colville-Andersen

Ukraine is on the verge of a new kind of mental health epidemic. The nation is grappling with PTSD in the wake of Russia's invasion in February 2022. Civilians have endured bombardment, and veterans returning from the front lines are deeply scarred. Traditional mental health services are overwhelmed, and often prioritize medication over therapy. The consequences of this unmet need are stark, with a troubling rise in domestic abuse.

Mikael Colville-Andersen, a Canadian–Danish urban designer, realized that the well-established concept of Nordic therapy gardens was relatively unknown outside of Denmark and Sweden. Driven by a profound belief in the healing power of these gardens, Mikael mobilized a team to create a pilot garden in Ukraine. Developed using research from the University of Copenhagen and extensive interviews with military veterans, the garden is designed to tackle mental trauma in multiple ways. It balances private, cocooning areas with communal spaces for sharing experiences and group therapy. The nature of warfare in Ukraine also informed the design, for instance drone attacks have left people with heightened anxiety and paranoia. In response, some cabins were designed with open roofs to provide a clear view of the sky, while others offer enclosed protection. Though initially conceived as a pilot project, the hope is that 'mental health professionals and landscape architects from other Ukrainian cities will come and learn about how the gardens work and open up important conversations about nature-based healing,' Mikael explains.

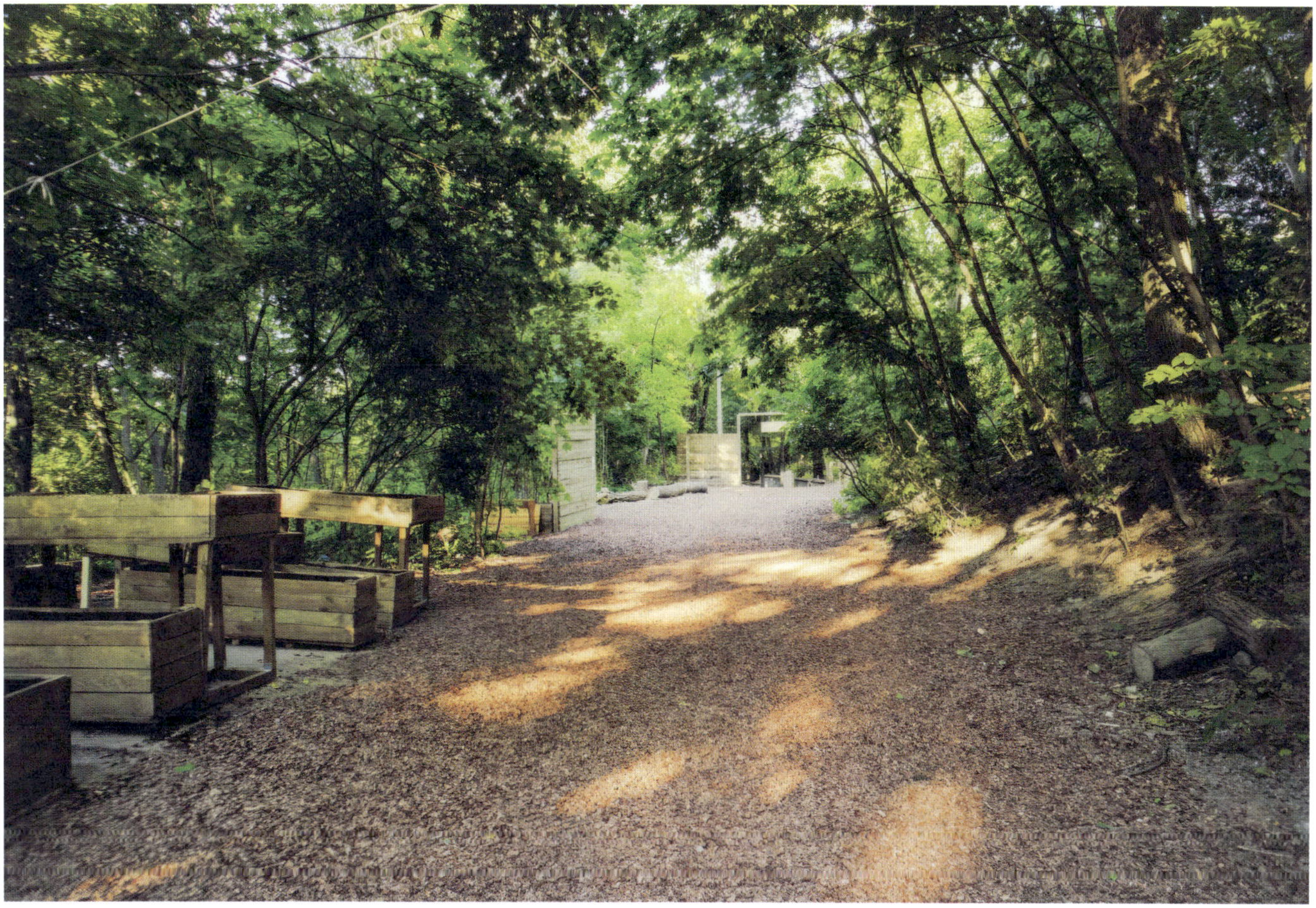

АЛЬТАНКА
Стежка до індивідуальної кабіни №4 –
для двох осіб.
Будь ласка, не підходьте, якщо вона зайнята.
ЗАЙНЯТО
ВІЛЬНО

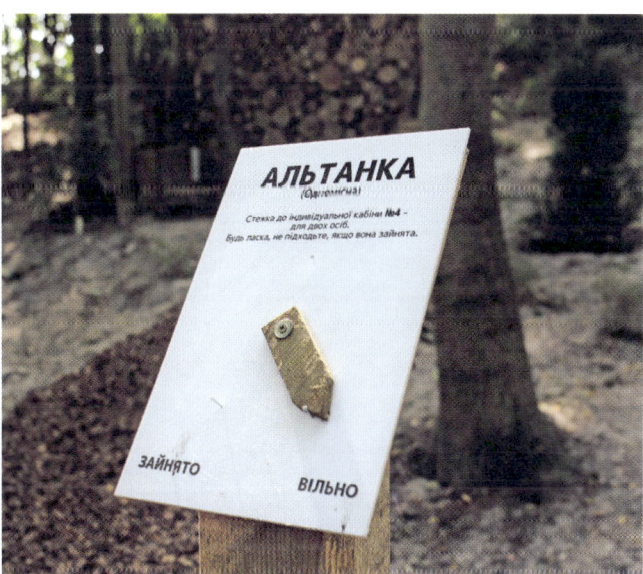

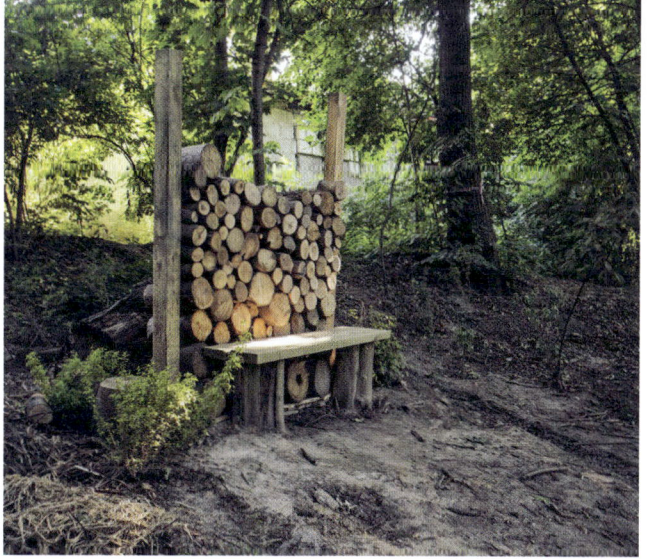

Tailor a healing garden to meet diverse health needs

Tager Home and Pamela Barnett Centre
Crowthorne, Berkshire, UK
Greenstone Design

The Tager Home caters for adults living with severe autism, a condition where sensory processing differences, such as hypersensitivity, hyposensitivity and sensory seeking, can profoundly impact daily life. Gayle Souter-Brown runs a garden design practice specializing in landscape architecture and urban design for health and wellbeing. It is a common misconception that all gardens are inherently 'healing' and beneficial to wellbeing. In reality, specific design features and strategies must be implemented to ensure gardens have a genuinely positive impact. This is especially crucial when catering to individuals with complex needs, such as those with autism.

The sensory garden at the Tagar Home is designed to be linear and predictable, minimizing overstimulation while incorporating plants to touch, smell and taste. A central raised bed serves as a sandpit for tactile interaction, allowing young people to sit within it, stand in it, or engage with it from the surrounding ground. The planters are made of smooth, planed (splinter-free) timber, providing a soft tactile experience. They also soften the acoustics (another source of over stimulation) to balance the use of concrete pavers on the main service path. The new planting includes a mix of non-toxic evergreen shrubs (*Pittosporum tenuifolium*), herbs such as rosemary (said to enhance cognitive function) and lavender (for its calming properties), and climbers like common jasmine (*Jasminum officinale*), which will soften the perimeter fence over time.

In direct contrast, the sensory garden at the Pamela Barnett home next door, which caters for adults living with severe learning disabilities, is designed for maximum stimulation. Visiting wildlife adds an element of surprise, complemented by six oak barrel ponds. Abundant mixed planting ensures year-round interest, with perennials and seasonal bulbs enhancing the sensory experience throughout spring and summer. These gardens demonstrate that healing gardens are far from a one-size-fits-all approach. Their design requires sensitivity and expertise to tailor features that offer the most beneficial effects for each user group, effects that go beyond promoting health, to actively treating illness.

REIM

AGINE

Imagination is a powerful tool, but *reimagining* demands more. It requires us to let go of the familiar and explore new paths. Inheriting complex systems and damaged landscapes, we face entrenched industries, opaque supply chains, and an intractable status quo. Challenging this can feel lonely, risky and deeply uncertain.

Gardens offer a unique space for experimentation, as they are microcosms where new ideas can safely take root. They are ancient sources of wisdom, long seen as living libraries and places of healing across cultures. Like forests for many Indigenous communities, gardens provide guidance and sustenance. Today, with higher stakes, they remain fertile ground for reimagining our path forwards.

Reimagining can take different forms. In a world of chronic over-supply and depleted natural resources, perhaps the most valuable and urgent form of reimagination lies in rethinking how we use what we already have. The world is changing at an alarming pace, and with each new era, something else becomes obsolete. This happens at every scale, from vast steel plants and quarries abandoned in favour of cheaper alternatives abroad, to materials in buildings or gardens that are no longer fit for purpose (or often just not fit for fashion). Where does all this redundant material go? How do you begin to dismantle a five-hectare power plant? And what happens to the local identity of the area now that its landmark coal factory has been abandoned? Gardens are helping us find answers to these questions. At Duisburg-Nord in the early 1990s, Latz + Partner unveiled an ambitious vision for an abandoned coal and steel plant, redefining what a post-industrial landscape could be. Their project remains one of the most significant of its kind, ushering in an era where derelict industrial spaces could be reimagined as places where nature and people coexist happily. On a domestic scale, waste is increasingly being viewed as a valuable resource in garden design. In Los Angeles, the landscape design studio Terremoto is using salvaged materials to develop a distinct local vernacular in the 'placeless' place that is LA. In lieu of a rich architectural heritage, repurposing the discarded brings a sense of locality to their gardens, rooting them in the environment – while reducing carbon impact in the process.

In Philadelphia and Essex, Apiary Studio and John Little respectively are investing in the skills required to reimagine waste materials. While these materials might be free, reworking them into something useful and beautiful is not.

We have become accustomed to uniformity and ease: paving that comes in neat right-angled slabs, bricks that slot together like a child's jigsaw. It takes considerable skill to reimagine cast-off materials in a manner that meets our aesthetic expectations – and a little re-education too. Clients are frequently surprised that the cost is higher, and need help buying into a less immaculate, less 'new' aesthetic.

Gardens can also act as a lens, helping us refocus. Sometimes this is quite literal – as in the Sky House in Vietnam, where MIA Design Studio invites us to look inwards rather than out, offering sanctuary within the dense fabric of Ho Chi Minh City. At other times, the shift in focus is about reframing. Floristry, for example, is traditionally associated with verdant life, celebrating plants at the blooming peak of their life cycle. But what if we widen the frame to include plants beyond this narrow snapshot in time? Florist Kitten Grayson does just that, creating sumptuous floral arrangements using dried plants and flowers, seed heads and other overlooked stages of the plant life cycle, as well as blooms, thereby expanding our understanding of what constitutes beauty and embracing a more complete narrative of nature's rhythms.

Gardens are famously good at helping us reframe our lives. The earth itself – *humus*, from the Latin for ground – quite literally grounds us. The combination of physical labour, the outdoors and tuning into the rhythms of nature can have a transformative effect on our health. And in the modern world, it can also help us reimagine ways of living. The permaculture movement reflects this shift, with practitioners all over the world. Some of them are simply adopting the holistic principles in their gardens at home, and some are using it as a complete framework for living. Outside Taipei, Yan-Han Tarng has created a permaculture farm and garden as an escape from city life, offering him and those who visit a chance to reconnect with a simpler, slower way of living.

While these gardens are finding new value in reimagining ancient and traditional practices, cutting-edge technology is helping us do the same, through a very different lens. As a tool-making, technologically driven species, we have always relied on innovation to bridge the gap between ourselves and the world. In our increasingly nature-deprived cities, can we use technology to reconnect with the natural world we so deeply need? And beyond that, could it help us reimagine greener futures and democratize access to gardens?

Glitch is a garden platform where users - garden-gamers and dreamers alike - can design and co-create virtual gardens using AI, machine-learning algorithms, AR and LiDAR. Elsewhere, AI-powered garden simulators are allowing home gardeners to plan and plant with a precision that once took years to learn (though not without some concern from traditional garden designers). Plant identification apps now place encyclopedic plant knowledge at our fingertips, previously only earned through years of study. It's all too easy to demonize technology and label it the enemy, but Kalpana Arias (profiled on page 96) challenges this false binary, urging us instead to see technology not just as a tool, but as an intelligent ally - one that can help us reconnect and reimagine our relationship with the living world.

At the other end of the spectrum, gardens help us look backwards to find future solutions. Swollen, extractive industries allowed to metastasize under capitalism need a radical rethink, perhaps one that involves returning to more traditional ways of doing things. Consider the fashion industry, one of the most toxic on the planet: it is the second-largest industrial polluter, accounting for 10% of global emissions. Reimagining this industry could unlock a big piece of the sustainability jigsaw puzzle. In Ireland and France, flax for linen is making a comeback. Farms that once lay dormant while we filled our wardrobes with polyester imported from China are finding new markets for plant-based textiles. Similarly, in the UK, commercial cultivation of plant-based dye is gaining traction as brands actively seek botanical alternatives to the toxic chemicals that have long dominated the industry. Through such initiatives, these regions are reimagining the world they inherited, gradually unravelling the intricate web of unsustainable practices we're all entangled in. Intelligence is the ability to adapt to change, and we either adapt, or we fail. Gardens present an incredible opportunity to explore models of adaptation that reverberate far beyond the garden gate. By creating space to experiment with *how* we garden, *what* we garden and *why* we grow, we open up the possibility to reimagine not just our landscapes, but our ways of living - for the better.

MIA Design Studio's Sky House in Ho Chi Minh → City, Vietnam, includes a garden on every level (pp.208-11).

Repurpose found materials from your own backyard

Space Barn
Apiary Studio, Philadelphia, USA
Martha Keen/Hans Hesselein

Many people talk about reimagining materials, but very few do it well or consistently. The reason for this is because it's hard. Our built world is designed for uniformity and efficiency, and reusing irregular and site-specific materials demands time, experimentation and skill, which are all costly commodities, especially for small businesses. But for Martha Keen and Hans Hesselein of Apiary Studio in Philadelphia, this challenge became a guiding principle. Making the ugly beautiful is central to their manifesto. Driven by a moral imperative to avoid waste, they have developed their craft over the past decade, honing techniques to turn rubble into rubies.

This project – a residential backyard on the site of an informal dump – was the perfect place to put their skills into practice. Granite paving slabs and concrete blocks salvaged from the site were laid to create a giant terrazzo-effect (see Glossary) terrace. The trick lies in the levelling: every fragment is a different depth and size, making the laying process a slow, laborious jigsaw puzzle. Stone from a nearby demolished church was repurposed to build a dry-stone wall and bench seating for the dining area. No virgin materials were used. The result is a garden that speaks to the local vernacular and forms a fitting extension to the passive house it surrounds.

Experiment with technology to fuel your imagination

Glitch
London, UK
Nowadays/Pitch Studios/Earthed Charity

Technology is often cast as the enemy – an obstacle between us and nature. If only children weren't so distracted by screens, if only adults weren't so tethered to the relentless ping of emails. But for technologist and guerrilla gardener Kalpana Arias and her team at Nowadays, technology and AI are not just tools, they are intellectual species with the potential to help us reconnect – and reimagine – an alternative future. Glitch is their cyber-gardening tool: a 'grow-to-play' version of guerrilla gardening designed to help a new generation reimagine urbanism for both people and planet. 'Designing a garden is an exercise in imagination,' Kalpana tells me, 'a space for speculative thinking that calls green-fingered vigilantes to action.' Through the Glitch platform, garden-gamers can design and co-create gardens using AI, machine-learning algorithms,

AR and LiDAR. As users interact with the platform, their input feeds a growing database that builds a garden based on both personal choices and local biodiversity. It's a novel, egalitarian and collaborative way of gardening that allows anyone to contribute – including people who might not have always found gardens accessible. It prompts people to ask: what kind of garden would I love to walk through? What should my street look like? Glitch is, at its heart, an act of imagination, which is one of the most underrated yet powerful tools we have when facing global uncertainty. It offers a way to visualize a different future, fuelling our imaginations about what's possible and invites new voices into a collaborative design partnership to grow a greener world – both online and off.

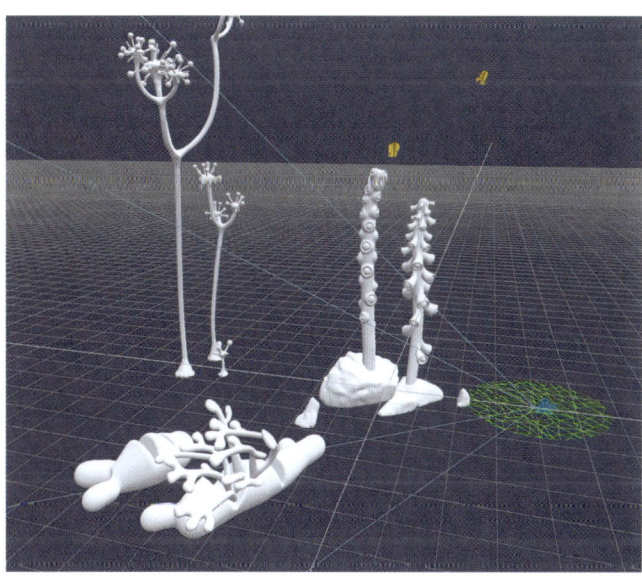

Integrate greening at every level for a home thrumming with life

Sky House
Ho Chi Minh City, Vietnam
MIA Design Studio

Ho Chi Minh City (formerly Saigon) is the most densely populated city in Vietnam, home to nearly nine million people, over seven million motorbikes and a skyline that evolves at breakneck speed, driven by some of the region's most ambitious urban infrastructure projects. Luxury high-rise offices and towering apartment blocks appear almost overnight, putting immense pressure on the city's already inadequate green spaces. Add in relentless humidity, pollution and city-wide construction, and the result is a toxic air quality that can feel oppressive and hard to escape. To compound things, development plots in Ho Chi Minh City leave little room for gardens and come in a standardized, narrow width. If you want more space, you have to build upwards. So how do you reconcile these constraints with a desire for greener urban living?

MIA Design Studio created a house where miniature gardens are woven into each of the multiple levels, transforming each floor into a pocket of greenery with lush vistas at every turn. Deep vertical wells flood the interiors with natural light, while trees and native planting placed in interconnecting rooms and landings can be seen from every room. The result is a building that no longer relies on its surrounding context – instead it has created its own internal landscape.

Celebrate the heritage of the site to create powerful public spaces

Landschaftspark Duisburg-Nord
Duisburg-Meiderich, Germany
Latz + Partner

What to do with a vast decommissioned steel plant? As cities and regions adapt to the decline of traditional industries like manufacturing, mining and steel production, the shift from industrial to post-industrial economies has left behind massive, vacant and abandoned industrial complexes. The site of Landschaftspark Duisburg-Nord was once a steel plant, which was decommissioned in the 1980s. Peter Latz won the design competition to transform the site thanks to his visionary approach of preserving the site's rich industrial heritage while reimagining it as a new model for urban parks. Central to the design intent was a desire to respect and highlight (rather than erase) the site's industrial legacy. Latz embraced the existing structures – blast furnaces, gas tanks and rail tracks – incorporating them as key features within the landscape.

Instead of demolishing these relics, they were repurposed. Concrete bunkers became spaces for a series of gardens; old gas tanks were transformed into pools for scuba divers; concrete walls were used by rock climbers; and in the centre of the site sits Piazza Metallica, a metamorphosis of the existing industrial structure into a public park. Even the contaminated soil underwent extensive remediation processes, including phytoremediation, rather than being replaced. Native vegetation was introduced alongside spontaneous plant growth, allowing nature to reclaim parts of the terrain organically. Landschaftspark Duisburg-Nord is a testament to the transformative power of innovative landscape architecture, showcasing how a site can be reimagined to honour its past, challenge traditional notions of a public park and inspire a generation about the potential of post-industrial sites to contribute to urban regeneration.

Experiment with materials and processes with biodiversity in mind

Hilldrop
Laindon, Essex, UK
John Little

Hilldrop is John Little's garden in Essex, which he bought in 1990 and has since become a test bed and playground for his experiments in waste. Using unwanted and unloved materials, he transforms them into thriving, functioning ecosystems. Little is something of a magician in this regard – no material is deemed too lowly, no corner of the garden too small, no animal or insect unworthy of a habitat. The results are inspiring and ecologically rich landscapes that are simultaneously low carbon, low cost and low maintenance (although not maintenance-free – see page 144). All it takes is a bit of imagination. And a dogged commitment to seeing the garden through a different lens, namely that of habitat creation.

For all these experiments and interventions, the goal is to boost biodiversity. When cladding the recording studio for his son in the garden, Little used sand as soundproofing since it also doubles as a nesting site for bees. A badly pruned weeping willow (not entirely accidentally) led to bark damage and created a better habitat for bugs. He removed all the fertile topsoil from a swathe of the garden and replaced it with crushed rubble, planting a brownfield meadow – the result is a higher proportion of insect life here than in other parts of the garden. A ring of tree stumps, known affectionately as the 'standing dead', provides a happy habitat for a range of invertebrates. Recently, a new 'Essex dry stone wall', made from builder's waste and rubble, serves as a beautiful and quotidian riff on the quintessential Cotswolds counterpart – and importantly, a perfect home for bees and other insects. John's garden is proof that reimagining materials has benefits that extend beyond saving stuff from the skip. It's a mindset, an art and quite possibly the future.

David Godshall Co-Founder of Terremoto

Californian landscape design company Terremoto has carved out its own path. Its approach is equal parts anarchic and deeply respectful – refreshingly radical in an industry that can feel steeped in stifling precedent. Woven into all their work is a sense of moral enquiry: a gentle and respectful interrogation of why we design gardens the way we do. Do these inherited norms still serve us? If not, why are we still doing it this way? The gardens they create are a testament to this questioning – a process that has evolved (and continues to evolve) in the years since David Godshall and his late business partner Alain Peauroi set up Terremoto.

Today, the company operates from offices in Los Angeles and San Francisco, with an illustrious and varied portfolio of projects that range from Frank Lloyd Wright masterpieces to lo-fi community projects. Despite the diversity, a clear thread runs through Terremoto's projects – one that goes beyond aesthetic to something more urgent and visceral: these gardens feel alive in ways that others don't.

This vitality stems from their non-conformist, 'respectfully inflammatory' approach to design, where rules are worn lightly (if at all) and everything is an evolving discussion. Design materializes and beauty 'emerges' in a process that feels radically different to traditional ways of making gardens. As David puts it: 'Recent historical patterns of garden-making mostly imposed beauty on a garden, or required beauty of a garden, whether through the geometry of French neoclassicism, to celebrate human supremacy over land, or the more pastoral English garden-making traditions. Even modern gardens are very much impositions of geometry on to land.' But the process at Terremoto allows for something else. 'We're using local materials, we're prioritizing ecology, we're not so fixed on drawing plans – and instead beauty emerges, rather than becomes imposed.'

For example, by setting yourself the constraint of using local or reused materials (which became a necessity during the pandemic), it 'expands your aesthetic imagination – that's the joy. Now we're building things that look different from anything we ever thought was possible'. A new vernacular emerges, along with economic resilience because you're not reliant on the global supply chain. In a similar way, a recent decision to stop building ground-up swimming pools – because it's just environmentally unjustifiable – has resulted in new solutions and responses that would never have been on the table had they not opened up that conversation. This might mean exploring an outdoor bathroom, or other ways to cool down in the heat of an LA summer – 'there are lots of options as long as people are open-minded about it'.

Another question they have begun asking is: how can we *do* less – not just how can we *use* less? How can we solve this design problem in the least number of moves? What's the smallest garden we can make that still satisfies the brief? Meaningfully reducing carbon footprint means more than swapping out materials for something local. 'As often as possible we try to come to peace with existing conditions,' says David. That might mean preserving an 'ugly' wall instead of replacing it, thereby saving materials, labour and carbon costs. 'Instead, we're asking, can we live with it?' Which becomes a radical design question. Alongside working on the process of finding new ways to make gardens, David and his team actively shine a light on the process itself. In the early days, with little completed work to show, they shared images of projects under construction. 'We just started being explicit about process and construction on our website and in the way that we portrayed our work,' David explains. The result? A candid, confident celebration of the garden-making journey – 'the guts' of it all. This transparency has had two powerful effects. Firstly, it is extremely refreshing in an industry that is obsessive about 'before and after' and the big reveal of the immaculate 'finished' garden. It speaks to the ongoing, never-ending reality of garden-making. They are living, breathing things that cannot and should not be seen as 'finished'. Secondly, these images made visible the people who were building their gardens. In California, it's mostly Latino immigrants who are building gardens and landscapes – by only showing the 'finished' garden at the end, you're 'rendering their contribution invisible'. Landscape architecture has a labour-acknowledgment problem (a problem not exclusive to the US) and Terremoto is working hard to make his visible. This involves early conversations with clients about paying labour teams appropriately and an internal working group to continually review how they can do better.

Yes, we've inherited flawed systems, but David remains optimistic. 'We seem to be awakening as a species to our global predicament. We have an opportunity to pivot and shift and do better. It's a great responsibility, but it's also super fun – what a time to be alive.'

Adopt a social enterprise model to care for the land and for people

PIGMENT Organic Dyes
Ashburton, South Devon, UK
Sophie Holt

The fashion industry is becoming increasingly aware of the environmental impact of its supply chains, particularly the toxicity of chemical dyes. However, awareness alone is not enough – brands need to find suppliers who can offer an alternative. Sophie Holt's small dye farm in Devon offers just that, providing a planet-friendly solution through organic plant dyes. Founded as a social enterprise, PIGMENT operates on a regenerative care-farming model, combining farming with therapeutic practices. Care farming uses farming practices to support people with health, social or educational needs, often as part of therapy, rehabilitation or special educational programmes. Just before having her daughter, Sophie discovered the world of natural dyeing, and realized there were no UK-grown organic natural dyes available. A long-standing desire to set up a care farm dovetailed perfectly with this revelation, leading to the creation of PIGMENT.

Care runs through the heart of the business at every level: care for the land through regenerative agriculture practices; for the planet by supplying the textile industry with sustainable alternatives; and for the people she supports working at the farm. These are largely neurodivergent young adults, individuals with learning difficulties and those who have experienced trauma. 'I'm really keen to advocate spaces that welcome all and meet the needs of all people, and that don't adhere to this capitalist way of working, [which ends up] isolating the people that need more support', she explains. This reimagining of what enterprise looks like transforms a small commercial dye garden into a 'wellness' exercise where 'people are learning to look after themselves through a connection with plants', as well as looking after the planet. PIGMENT is proof that if we reimagine our way of working, supplying sustainable alternatives to a once-toxic industry can benefit both people and the planet.

Replace roads with rivers to regenerate life and cool city air

Cheonggyecheon Stream
Seoul, South Korea
Seo-Ahn Total Landscape

Cheonggyecheon Stream has been the key artery through the South Korean capital for centuries. Its recent transformation from a polluting concrete highway into a vibrant watercourse marks a full-circle return to the vital waterway and cultural corridor it once was in the 14th century. For much of the last hundred years, urban planning around the world prioritized making cities work for cars, resulting in decaying, lifeless concrete environments, blanketed and airless with smog and pollution. Today, the mission is to make these cities more liveable for humans.

What's particularly interesting about this poster-child project is that the highway wasn't replaced; it was simply removed from the road network. The site was reimagined as a human-orientated, ecological space, one that has brought life back to the heart of Seoul – human, vegetal and wild. The transformation has reshaped the city. According to studies by the Seoul Institute, the area around the stream is now 3.6 °C (6.5 °F) cooler than nearby streets. The removal of the highway created channels of airflow through the city, improving air circulation, with nitrogen dioxide levels falling by 35%.

Wildlife has returned as well: a 2022 survey by the Seoul Institute found 666 species in the area, including 174 animal species and 492 plant species. Reimaging a city with fewer cars not only removes the pollution and the concrete, but also revitalizes everything else around it.

Observe the natural rhythm of nature with dried flowers

Kitten Grayson Flowers
Somerset, UK
Kitten Grayson

Large-scale flower cultivation is often resource-intensive, relying heavily on water – particularly in regions already facing water shortages, like parts of Kenya and Colombia – and dependent on chemical fertilizers and pesticides, which can degrade soil health and contaminate local water sources. Add to that the carbon footprint of refrigeration and air freight required to maintain the freshness of flowers across global supply chains, and the environmental toll becomes clear.

Over the course of the past decade, however, there's been a blossoming shift and growing demand for locally grown, seasonal and environmentally responsible floristry, a trail Kitten Grayson has been blazing for double that time. More recently, this ethos has evolved into a new-found appreciation for dried or 'everlasting' flowers, largely grown biodynamically from Kitten's small flower farm in Somerset. 'Dried flowers offer

a thoughtful alternative, reducing waste and allowing us to create lasting, textural arrangements that change with the seasons,' Kitten explains. 'It's a way of celebrating the cycles of nature while embracing a more mindful, considered approach to floristry.' By growing her flowers biodynamically, Kitten builds a deeper connection to the land, ensuring they are 'nurtured with deep respect for the natural rhythms of the earth, supporting not just healthy soil, but biodiversity and long-term sustainability. This approach is at the heart of everything I do, allowing me to create designs that are truly connected to nature.' This new model of floristry invites us to reimagine the beauty in every stage of a plant's life cycle, and in doing so builds a more authentic relationship with nature – and gives something back to her in return.

Protect traditional crafts by commissioning skilled artisans

The Newt
Bruton, Somerset, UK
Koos and Karen Bekker

In the words of celebrated gardener and broadcaster Monty Don, a garden like this only comes along once in a lifetime. Such is the detail and extravagance of the gardens at The Newt, a working estate in South Somerset, UK, lovingly given a new lease of life by South African businessman Koos Bekker and his wife Karen, a former editor-in-chief of *Elle Decor* in South Africa. Since purchasing Hadspen House in 2013, the couple has spent the intervening years transforming the house and gardens into a modern working estate, hotel and cider farm.

What sets The Newt apart is not just the 500 varieties of apple tree, the extraordinarily productive gardens, or the expansive formal landscaping, but the unwavering commitment to craft. Across the estate's 800 acres, the hand of the maker is everywhere. Immaculate stonemasonry stretches as far as the eye can see, a testament to spectacular finesse and skill. Hazel hurdlers (see Glossary) have woven miles of sinuous, sculptural fencing walls. Apples are trained into double helixes and perfect espaliers wrap around the restored parabola. In a glistening Wyvern cave, crushed shells line the paths, and hand-turned oak walkways lead visitors through an immersive, otherworldly space.

This level of detail requires deep pockets but, more importantly, deep respect for traditional skills and their survival. These crafts, honed and passed down through generations of makers, speak intimately of place, yet many are at risk of dying out. Reimagining the garden as a place to celebrate these skills is both an act of extraordinary privilege and profound generosity. These are living arts – supporting livelihoods, sustaining local economies, preserving cultural heritage and leaving a legacy for future generations. Gardens like this may only come along once in a lifetime – but when they do, we are all the richer for it.

Radically rethink what makes a garden

Museum Garden
California, USA
Terremoto

'When we look to history, we observe that gardens are expressions of the culture and values of the societies from which they emerge.' So says US-based garden makers Terremoto. But the culture we've inherited, they argue, is exploitative, materially consumptive, and places value on the wrong things. This realization has prompted a new way of doing things, one that requires a review of all aspects of garden-making.

One of the key outcomes of this process is the belief that old and new must coexist. 'The erasure of the previous landscape in service of the new is a bogus mechanism of a colonizing culture,' they say – a practice that disconnects us from the history of both the land and the project itself. Embracing what exists not only creates deeper continuity, it also brings us closer to a closed material loop, dramatically reducing the need for new inputs. In this garden, that meant keeping the 'ugly' walls and existing hard structures, and finding thoughtful ways to bridge the gap between what the garden was and what the

garden needs to be. Simple interventions – like a ladder to link the spaces, a low-fi pergola to sit under and enjoy the view, and reusing on-site materials to 'blur the ruins into pavers, paths and places to sit' – bring the site gently and intelligently into the present.

Another product of Terremoto's radical re-evaluation of garden-making is the rejection, where possible, of irrigation systems. While this has clear ecological and environmental benefits – reduced water use, for one – it also fosters something more profound. 'A client who is willing to hand-water the garden will connect with the garden physically, emotionally and spiritually. Because they are responsible for it, they will care for it, learn to care for the land and become a gardener.' And so in this garden, despite the climate and the challenging topography, the clients do exactly that. In caring for the garden by hand, they are not just tending plants, they are reimagining what it means to be stewards of the land.

Elise Van Middelem Entrepreneur and Founder of SUGi

Elise Van Middelem is in 'the business of awe' – conjuring life in unlikely places, on land that has been written off and neglected, assumed too poor to support plants, let alone forests. But thanks to a little-known forestry method and a global network of forest makers, SUGi, the non-profit Elise started in 2019, has created almost 250 pocket forests in 52 cities on 6 continents and reconnected almost 80,000 people to nature in just 5 years. And despite the incredible growth – literal and metaphorical – Elise is still awed by the transformation a pocket forest can bring to both the land and the community they're in – 'it's like magic'.

Elise grew up surrounded by nature. Her father still farms the land she grew up on in Belgium. While working in San Francisco as an adult, she would regularly escape the city to the ancient redwood forest to calm her nervous system, increasingly aware how vital this was for her wellbeing. But it wasn't until much later, after years of working with luxury brands, that an idea for a career change began to formulate in Elise's mind. She was working on creative brand strategies for luxury clients, and lots of the conversation was focused on how to deliver impact and awareness. Like many of us, Elise felt overwhelmed with the complex ecological problems we were facing and the constant talk of awareness. 'One day I just thought we don't need more awareness, we need action,' Elise tells me.

That action came from a serendipitous phone call with a friend in Jodhpur in India, who had recently seen a YouTube video on Miyawaki forestry, a technique that Elise had become interested in. The friend had used it to transform land in India into a thriving biodiverse ecosystem. Before long the idea took shape. The Miyawaki method of planting high-density native-only forests was the perfect way to tackle so many of the problems Elise had been thinking about – climate resilience, biodiversity loss and fractured communities. It was tangible, it delivered results and it could be applied anywhere in the world. A successful pilot project in Beirut followed shortly after and they were off.

Today, the core mission remains the same – planting pocket forests to provide climate resilience, help nature recover and restore social bonds in a fractured world. To do this, SUGi has mobilized an army of forest makers, trained in the Miyawaki method and funded by SUGi, to create forests in their community. SUGi has tapped into a global hunger for a closer relationship with nature: 'People desperately want to be part of the solution but lack the tools and the means to do it'. When SUGi planted its first pocket forest in New York, over 400 volunteers turned up to help and so far over 80,000 people have been involved in planting SUGi forests worldwide.

The benefit to the environment is plain to see, and SUGi is a meticulous data collector and publishes a pioneering Impact Report each year, making its gains visible, accessible and measurable. In London, fungi usually only found in old forests have been observed in pocket forests only a few years old. In Cameroon the forest is helping to maintain the underground water supply and in India, fragile desert ecosystems have been restored.

But they are also delivering a host of social benefits. In Colombia, food forests of papaya, cacao and moringa are bolstering food security. In Cape Town, pocket forests are reconnecting Khoi First Nations communities with land and species they were separated from during apartheid, while also addressing the structural inequity of access to green space. And across India, outdoor classrooms are transforming education, connecting children to nature while providing shade, beauty and hands-on environmental learning.

Perhaps the greatest achievement, however, is the restoration of hope. SUGi's forests offer tangible proof that nature will return – and that we, too, can find our way back to it when given the tools, time and space. For Elise, there is a 'transcending poetry' in these forests, one that surpasses geography and culture. 'Woven throughout our forests is the resilience of the human heart and imagination, which will always be our muse.'

Nourish soil and skin through biodynamic practices

Weleda Medicinal Gardens
Derbyshire, UK/Schwäbisch Gmünd, Germany
Weleda

Skincare and soil may not sound like obvious bedfellows, but at Weleda they're intimately linked. Founded in 1921 by Rudolf Steiner initially as a pharmaceutical laboratory with its own garden, it has evolved into a global leader in natural skincare and today it sells a tube of its iconic Skin Food (first formulated in 1926) every eight seconds. Over its hundred-year history, one vital constant has been growing ingredients organically, using biodynamic methods. It is how they guarantee quality and purity – 'looking after the soil and farming biodynamically is how we produce the most potent plant actives for our products, so that our finished products really deliver on promise,' explains Weleda UK's Managing Director, Jayn Sterland.

And fundamental to healthy plants is healthy soil. In biodynamic farming, beds and fields are cultivated in a soil-friendly way, without synthetic or chemical fertilizers. Instead natural preparations made with crops grown specifically for this purpose are used, and crops are sown in sync with the biodynamic calendar in a system that sees the farm and garden as a self-sustaining ecosystem. In the UK alone, Weleda cultivates around forty-five plant species this way, for medicines and natural cosmetics, and they save seeds from twenty-three plant species for cultivation the following year (other plants are propagated from cuttings, or are perennials). Such care and attention makes the soils resilient and rich in humus, allowing them to better cope with extreme conditions such as wetness or drought. And means they produce healthier plants.

This commitment to a holistic way of thinking, the deep understanding that the microbiomes of both the soil and of our skin are linked, takes a level of care you'd think would be at odds with a commercially viable global skincare brand. And while it's true that hand-picking crops and growing biodynamically is not the cheap option, Jayn explains that in 'true cost' accounting, these ingredients give back far more than they cost the planet – 'we believe this is how every business should operate, responsibly, sustainably, ethically and for the long-term'.

Aside from producing precious plant tinctures, Weleda's gardens also support the business in other ways – 'for example in Derbyshire we host meetings, talks, workshops and open days at our gardens, as well as a forest school for local schoolchildren to introduce them to the wonder of nature and to encourage a sense of connection with the landscape and a growing awareness of the seasons'. The gardens also provide a place for staff to relax and learn about the plants, their qualities and the role they play in their products. And they're proof that placing nature at the heart of your business is not just good for us and the planet, but can be good for business too.

Seek beauty in forgotten places

Giardino dell'Impossibile
Favignana, Italy
Mariella Gabriella Campo

An abandoned quarry is something of a scar on the landscape, an open sore laying bare our shameless extraction of the Earth's resources. The limestone quarry of Favignana, off the coast of Sicily, was once a vital source of 'tufa' limestone, used to build much of Sicily's most cherished landmarks. For centuries, it was a pillar of the local economy until the 1950s, when its operations ceased. That could have been the end of the story, if it weren't for the ambitious vision of Maria Gabriella Campo, who saw the quarry not as an eyesore, but as an opportunity to express her great love for the island and her growing passion for botany. Not for nothing is it called the Impossible Garden. This precipitous subterranean site has been developed in stages over the past sixty years on barren, stony soil. The four-hectare garden is a microclimate unto itself, where the towering inner walls of the quarry trap air at a steady, ideal temperature for plant life.

Today, the garden boasts over 500 species of plants, including notable collections of hibiscus, frangipani and water lilies. The steep gorges and caves, once used by quarry workers to rest and have lunch in the shade, stand as a testament to the site's previous incarnation. The *Giardino dell'Impossibile* is a surreal, idiosyncratic tribute to both Maria's resilience and determination, and the Mediterranean species that have happily made a home here against impossible odds.

Honour cultural identity with collected plants

Parque Lineal
Mexico City, Mexico
Fernanda Rionda

In Mexico, trains are often used for freight, not passengers, and the people who work on them, the *ferrocarrileros*, spend most of their lives on them, a nomadic existence ferrying goods across the country's 24,000-kilometre (15,000-mile) rail network. Along their travels, they collect plants – botanical curiosities, living souvenirs and species that remind them of home. These are often *nopales* (prickly pear or tender cactus pads), eaten raw or used in soups, salads and stews.

Mexican landscape architect Fernanda Rionda had a long-standing relationship with Ferromex, Mexico's largest rail consortium, and was asked to improve an awkward strip of land between two buildings – a place workers formerly had to make a twenty-five minute detour to reach. The site, a narrow corridor running alongside the railway, wasn't an obvious place for a garden, but Fernanda saw this as an opportunity.

Inspired by the *ferrocarrileros* and their plant collections, she designed a garden that pays homage to the rich ecology of Mexico's industrial landscapes. Planted with native species, including many of the *nopales* gathered by railway workers, the space has been transformed from a disused industrial area into a dynamic plant community – a living landscape rich in cultural identity and place. Using existing recycled and industrial materials together with strong graphic lines that echo those of the railway tracks, Fernanda created not just a new shortcut for the railway workers, but an immersive garden that celebrates a little-known facet of Mexican culture. What was previously invisible work has been given an identity in the garden, offering the *ferrocarrileros* a renewed sense of pride in both their work and the country's rich and varied plant life.

Return to seasonal ways of working as a salve for modern life

Yamana Garden
Yangmingshan Mountain
Yan-Han Tarng

Yamana Garden is a residential permaculture farm outside Taipei, established by Yan-Han Tarng in 2002. Like many professionals in developed Southeast Asian cities, Yan-Han's lifestyle was fraught and finely balanced. He was a senior telecoms executive living in the city, working long hours with little work–life harmony. At first, the goal of the project was to restore a healthier work–life balance, reconnect with the land and live harmoniously with nature. While all those things remain central, the garden has grown into something even more transformative: a space for reimagining how we live and 'learning to live with inconvenience'.

The garden is designed according to the traditional Chinese solar calendar. In spring, the soil is prepared for planting, rice seedlings are transplanted, and plums are harvested to make plum wine, plum vinegar and pickled plums. In summer, shelters are built and soy ploughing takes place, and in winter, it's time to make sour lime tea, roast coffee beans and ferment vanilla beans. These so-called 'inconveniences' are actually building something powerful – a deeper resilience and connection to the land. Throughout the year, tofu and bread are also made, and visitors are welcomed for short day courses or longer-term stays. This provides an opportunity for people to explore alternative lifestyles, reflect during a life crossroads, or learn self-sufficiency skills.

Over the years, Yan-Han has become less anxious and no longer fears not having enough. 'In the societal system, when a water pipe breaks, you'd think it's the plumber's responsibility, and you pay them to fix it. At Yamana Garden, I see problems and learn how to solve them, not relying on money to take care of everything. At Yamana, I chop firewood and cook with it. The wood is a readily available resource, unlike in the societal system, where people think they can only rely on paying for gas to cook.' Yamana Garden and its community exemplify a different way of living, where the principles of permaculture equip you with everything you truly need, not what you think you need.

Glossary

AquiPor: A permeable concrete that helps mitigate flood risks by allowing rainwater to pass through it, rather than pooling on the surface and causing flooding. It also uses low-carbon cement that requires a fraction of the energy to produce it and emits much less CO_2 than traditional concrete, making it an extremely valuable material for the future infrastructure of our cities.

Biodiversity: The variety and variability of life on Earth, encompassing the diversity of species, genetic variation within those species, and the range of ecosystems they form. High biodiversity supports healthy, resilient environments by maintaining ecological balance, enabling natural processes such as pollination, nutrient cycling and climate regulation, and providing resources for human wellbeing.

Biodynamic: A holistic, ecological and ethical approach to farming, gardening, food and nutrition, developed in the 1920s by Austrian philosopher and scientist Rudolf Steiner. It emphasizes soil health and biodiversity, viewing the farm as a self-sustaining ecosystem and living organism. Biodynamics works with the rhythms of the moon and celestial cycles to guide planting and sowing according to the biodynamic calendar. Specific practices and preparations, such as horn manure (cow manure fermented in a buried cow horn) and compost teas made from plants like yarrow and dandelion, are integral to the system. Similar to organic certification, farms practising biodynamics can also become accredited.

Coir/coco-peat: Coconut coir is made from the fibres between the shell and outer covering of coconuts. The shorter fibres are an excellent growing medium and alternative to peat-based composts.

Composting: Even those with small gardens can reap the benefits of composting, which serves the dual purpose of repurposing organic waste and enriching soil. From counter-top composters and hot-bins to larger community composting facilities, it's one of the easiest ways to reduce your carbon footprint by diverting waste from landfills, which produce greenhouse gases.

Ecological succession: The natural process of change in an ecosystem's species composition over time, occurring in stages as plants, animals and microorganisms establish, interact and modify their environment. It can be **primary** (on barren land) or **secondary** (after disturbances), and eventually leads to a stable and biodiverse ecosystem.

Encouraging complexity: A gardening or ecological principle that promotes biodiversity and resilience by incorporating diverse plant species, layers and habitats. This approach enhances ecosystem functions, supports wildlife and improves soil health by mimicking natural environments.

AquiPor

Coir/coco-peat

Ecological succession

Gabion

Food forest: A sustainable agricultural system designed to mimic the structure and biodiversity of a natural forest. It integrates a variety of edible plants, including fruit and nut trees, shrubs, herbs, vegetables and ground covers, all working together in layers. These layers – canopy, understory, shrubs, ground covers, vines and root crops – create a self-sustaining ecosystem that supports soil health, biodiversity and water retention. Once established, food forests require minimal maintenance and provide a diverse, year-round harvest. Often used in permaculture, they promote resilience, environmental stewardship and local food security, offering an eco-friendly approach to food production.

Gabion: A great way of building walls and making use of excess materials, using steel-mesh baskets filled with stone, rock or rubble. They're low-tech and easy to erect and give projects an industrial look, while also providing excellent habitats for insects, reptiles and small mammals. They can be planted with rock-loving plants or topped with grass.

Gravel and permeable surfaces: Permeable surfaces allow for water drainage, mitigating against flooding and allowing for self-seeding, which increases biodiversity and reduces the risk of urban heat islands (UHIs). Gravel also reduces the need for resource-heavy materials such as concrete hard-standings and mortar.

Green roof: Buildings with a flat roof, or even smaller structures like bike stores and sheds, can be transformed into habitats for insects and pollinators. Pre-seeded meadow or sedum turf is available to simply roll out on to flat surfaces, providing there is a fall to allow water runoff.

Ground cover: Low-growing plants that spread across the soil, reducing erosion, retaining moisture, and suppressing weeds. Often used in landscaping and permaculture, they include grasses, clover, creeping perennials and native species that improve soil health and biodiversity.

Guerrilla gardening: Planting and cultivating land in neglected or public spaces without official permission, with the goal of beautifying urban areas, improving biodiversity, and raising environmental and social awareness. Often done in vacant parcels of land, roadsides or abandoned properties, it transforms underutilized spaces into green, productive, active and ecologically rich environments.

Habitat: The natural environment where a species lives, providing essential resources such as food, water, shelter and breeding sites. Healthy habitats support biodiversity, ecological balance and species survival.

Green roof

Hügelkultur

Miyawaki forestry

No-dig veg beds

Hazel or willow supports: Structures made from flexible hazel or willow branches, used to support climbing plants like beans, peas and flowers. They're eco-friendly, biodegradable and look lovely, blending naturally into gardens and can be woven into arches, trellises or plant frames.

Healing garden: A garden designed to promote physical, emotional and psychological wellbeing through interaction with nature. Often found in hospitals, therapy centres and eco-resorts or health spas, these gardens use sensory elements like plants, water and pathways to reduce stress, enhance recovery and foster relaxation.

Hügelkultur: A raised-bed gardening method that layers logs, branches, leaves and soil. As the wood decays, it retains moisture, releases nutrients and enriches soil, reducing the need for watering and fertilizing.

Miyawaki forestry: A reforestation method by Dr Akira Miyawaki that plants dense, layered native species (3-5 saplings/m²) to mimic natural forests. This accelerates growth, creating self-sustaining forests in 20-30 years instead of a century, often in urban or degraded areas.

Native species: Plants (or animals) that have evolved naturally in a specific region over time without human introduction. They are well-adapted to local climate, soil and ecosystems, supporting biodiversity by providing food and habitats for native wildlife while requiring less maintenance, water and fertilizers than non-native species.

No-dig veg beds: A gardening method where soil is left undisturbed, reducing compaction, preserving beneficial microbes and minimizing weed growth. Layers of organic matter, such as compost, mulch or cardboard, are placed on top to suppress weeds, improve fertility and increase water retention - all without the need for tilling.

Non-native/invasive: A non-native species is introduced to an ecosystem outside its natural range. An invasive species spreads aggressively, out-competing native organisms, disrupting ecological balance and harming biodiversity, often due to a lack of natural predators or controls in the new environment.

Old paving slabs/stones: These can be broken down and used as gabion walls, which can be used as seating or to zone your garden. The open structure means that it will quickly become an ideal habitat for insects and encourage self-seeding plants to make their home there.

Non-native/invasive

Permaculture

Rammed earth

Seed bombs

Permaculture: A design system that mimics natural ecosystems to create self-sufficient agricultural and living environments. It integrates land, resources, people and the environment through regenerative practices like agroforestry, water conservation and biodiversity, promoting resilience and ecological harmony.

Planting community: A group of plant species that naturally grow together in a specific environment, supporting each other through complementary growth habits, resource sharing and ecological functions. Used in ecological landscaping and permaculture for resilience and biodiversity.

Rammed earth: An ancient building method where clay and aggregates are compressed in layers within a mould to form strong, naturally insulating walls with a warm, organic appearance.

Rewilding: The process of restoring ecosystems to their natural, self-sustaining state by allowing native species, habitats and natural processes to recover, often with minimal human intervention.

Salutogenic: An approach to health and wellbeing that focuses on factors that promote physical, mental and social resilience rather than just preventing or treating disease. It emphasizes positive lifestyle choices, environmental influences and psychological strengths that contribute to overall wellness and the ability to cope with stress.

Seed bombs: Small balls made of clay, compost and seeds, designed for easy dispersal in neglected or hard-to-reach areas. Used in guerrilla gardening and ecological restoration, they protect seeds from predators and harsh conditions, allowing plants to establish themselves and contribute to reforestation, pollinator support and urban greening.

Seed collecting: The practice of gathering, drying and storing seeds from plants for future planting, conservation or breeding. It supports biodiversity, preserves heirloom varieties and enables rewilding, ecological restoration and sustainable agriculture.

Sensory garden: A designed outdoor space that engages all five senses - sight, smell, touch, taste and hearing - through diverse plants, textures, fragrances and sounds. It promotes relaxation, therapy and learning, benefiting individuals with sensory impairments, autism or stress-related conditions by providing a calming and immersive natural experience.

Seed collecting

Sensory garden

Succession planting

SuDS (Sustainable Drainage Systems)

Succession planting: A gardening technique where crops are planted in stages or in quick succession to ensure continuous harvests. It maximizes space and productivity by replacing harvested plants with new ones, extending the growing season and optimizing land use.

SuDS (Sustainable Drainage Systems): Water management systems that mimic natural drainage to reduce urban flooding, improve water quality and enhance biodiversity. They include rain gardens, green roofs, permeable pavements and wetlands, promoting sustainable water use and resilience in cities.

Terracotta: An ancient material that shouldn't be overlooked. Warm in texture and tone, it can be used for paving, walling and containers. When laid on edge, it creates a permeable, highly decorative floor finish, and as pots, it offers a reusable alternative to ever-pervasive plastic.

Terrazzo: Terrazzo is a composite material made from waste like stone, glass, marble chips or plastic set in cement and precast into slabs. Used for flooring and outdoor furniture such as tabletops or seating.

Vermiculture: A technique using earthworms to turn organic waste into nutrient-rich vermicompost, boosting soil fertility and plant growth while recycling food scraps. It's simple to set up at home: use a ventilated plastic tub with shredded paper, cardboard and food scraps, then add red wigglers (*Eisenia foetida*). Keep the bin moist and feed regularly - within 2-3 months, you'll have rich, dark compost full of nutrients.

Weed: Any plant growing where it's unwanted, competing with cultivated plants for resources. They may be native or non-native, beneficial or harmful, and their classification is often subjective.

Wildlife corridors: Natural or constructed pathways that connect fragmented habitats, allowing animals to move safely between them. They preserve biodiversity by enabling species to migrate, find mates, access food and adapt to environmental changes. These corridors can be green belts, hedgerows, riverbanks or purpose-built crossings over and under roads. By reducing habitat fragmentation from human activities, they maintain genetic diversity, support ecosystem health and ensure the long-term survival of species.

Terracotta

Terrazzo

Vermiculture

Wildlife corridors

Border of autumn perennials and grasses in Lianne Pot's prairie garden in the Netherlands. →
Miscanthus sinensis, Pennisetum messaicum **'Red Bunny Tails'**, *Aster, Helenium* **'Waltraut'**, *Rudbeckia fulgida, Monarda* **'Scorpion'** and *Veronica* **'Fascination'**.

Bibliography

Bailey, Fran. *The Healing Power of Plants*. Pop Press, 2019.

Blom, Jinny. *The Thoughtful Gardener*. Frances Lincoln, 2017.

Blom, Jinny. *What Makes a Garden*. Frances Lincoln, 2023.

Cluitmans, Laurie, ed. *On the Necessity of Gardening: An ABC of Art, Botany and Cultivation*. Valiz, 2021.

Dunnett, Nigel. *Naturalistic Planting Design: The Essential Guide*. Filbert Press, 2019.

Dunnett, Nigel, and James Hitchmough, eds. *The Dynamic Landscape: Design, Ecology and Management of Naturalistic Urban Planting*. Routledge, 2004.

Farrell, Marchelle. *Uprooting: From the Caribbean to the Countryside – Finding Home in an English Garden*. Canongate Books, 2023.

Harpignies, J. P., ed. *Visionary Plant Consciousness: The Shamanic Teachings of the Plant World*. Park Street Press, 2007.

Howard, Ebenezer. *Garden Cities of To-morrow*. CreateSpace Independent Publishing Platform, 2016.

Jellicoe, Geoffrey and Susan Jellicoe. *The Landscape of Man*. Thames & Hudson, 1979.

Johnson, Dr Ayana Elizabeth. *What If We Get It Right?: Visions of Climate Futures*. Random House, 2024.

Kingsbury, Noel and Claire Takacs. *Wild: The Naturalistic Garden*. Phaidon, 2022.

Klein, Naomi. *This Changes Everything: Capitalism vs. the Climate*. Allen Lane, 2014.

Laing, Olivia. *The Garden Against Time: In Search of a Common Paradise*. Picador, 2024.

Massey, Tom. *RHS Resilient Garden*. DK, 2023.

Miles, Ellen, ed. *Nature Is a Human Right*. DK, 2022.

Moore, Darryl. *Gardening in a Changing World: Plants, People and the Climate Crisis*. Pimpernel Press, 2022.

Mullet, Carolyn. *Adventures in Eden: An Intimate Tour of the Private Gardens of Europe*. Timber Press, 2020.

Rainer, Thomas and Claudia West. *Planting in a Post-Wild World: Designing Plant Communities for Resilient Landscapes*. Timber Press, 2018.

Sheldrake, Merlin. *Entangled Life: How Fungi Make Our Worlds, Change Our Minds & Shape Our Futures*. The Bodley Head, 2020.

Snow, Lalage. *War Gardens: A Journey Through Conflict in Search of Calm*. Quercus, 2018.

Souter-Brown, Gayle. *Landscape and Urban Design for Health and Well-Being*. Routledge, 2014.

Stuart-Smith, Sue. *The Well Gardened Mind*. William Collins, 2020.

Subramaniam, Banu. *Botany of Empire: Plant Worlds and the Scientific Legacies of Colonialism (Feminist Technosciences)*. University of Washington Press, 2024.

Takacs, Claire, with Giacomo Guzzon. *Visionary: Gardens and Landscapes for our Future*. Hardie Grant Books, 2024.

Pih, Darren. *Radical Landscapes: Art, Identity and Activism*. Tate Publishing, 2022.

Tree, Isabella. *Wilding: The Return of Nature to a British Farm*. Picador, 2018.

Walton, Samantha. *Everybody Needs Beauty: In Search of the Nature Cure*. Bloomsbury Circus, 2021.

Wellcome Collection. *This Book Is a Plant: How to Grow, Learn and Radically Engage with the Natural World*. Profile Books, 2022.

Willis, Kathy. *Good Nature: The New Science of How Nature Improves Our Health*. Bloomsbury, 2024.

Wilson, Edward O. *Biophilia: The human bond with other species*. Harvard University Press, 1984.

Yudina, Anna. *Garden City: Supergreen Buildings, Urban Skyscapes and the New Planted Space*. Thames & Hudson, 2017.

Acknowledgments

A huge thank you to Augusta, my wonderful editor at Thames & Hudson, for appearing in my inbox two years ago and hovering reassuringly nearby ever since. It's been a total pleasure to turn this idea into a book. I have you to thank for sowing that first seed and offering a steady stream of gentle guidance and support ever since. Thanks also to my friend and agent Anna, who swept in at the eleventh hour to handle all the things I can't and be a voice of measured calm in the predictable moments of overwhelm. There have been many others who have helped with the watering and nurturing of *Gardens That Can Save the World* – Frank, Yasmin, Natalia and the rest of the team at Thames & Hudson who have patiently nudged and prodded, sourced images, corralled permissions forms, caught balls I dropped, humoured indecision on book covers and lent years of expertise to a first-timer with slightly delusional time-management skills.

Despite the self-inflicted stress of squeezing the writing of this in and around work and family, it has been a quietly life-changing experience. It's confirmed to me beyond all doubt that the world is a wonderful place, full of people who want to make it even better. They've shown me that hope is a discipline, one we can all practise. Thank you all for so generously sharing your work with me. And a special extra thanks to Isabella, someone I admire and respect so much and whose life and work are the message of the book made manifest.

Finally thank you to my resident eternal optimist Doug, for (among many other things) your belief that it's brightening up – I think you could be right. And to the little housemates we live with, this and everything in this book is for you and all your generation.

Picture credits

a = above; b = below; c = centre; l = left; r = right

2 Natalia Price-Cabrera
7 Lia Brazier
9 Evan Sklar / Alamy Stock Photo
12–13 Rick Bowden / Loop Images / Universal Images Group via Getty Images
14–15 Peter Horree / Alamy Stock Photo
16–17 Vizerskaya / Getty Images
20 Ximena Nazal
23 Phillip Johnson Landscapes
24–25 Estudio Ome
26–29 Finbarr Fallon
30–33 Alexa Hoyer
34 Dimitar Harizanov
35l, 35ar Giovanni Nardi
35br Dimitar Harizanov
36 Harry Stuart-Smith
38, 39a, 39bl, 40–41 Charlie Harpur
39br Charlie Burrell
42 Siegfried Layda / Getty Images
43l Simon Turner / Alamy Stock Photo
43ar, 43br Rick Darke
44–45 Lim Weixiang / Zeitgeist Photos
46 Kari Ahlers / Alamy Stock Photo
47l Ernst Wrba / Alamy Stock Photo
47ar Mauritius Images GmbH / Alamy Stock Photo
47br Ernst Wrba / Alamy Stock Photo
48–51 Ximena Nazal
52–53 Nigel Dunnett
54 Phillip Handforth
55al SLA Architects
55bl Phillip Handforth
55r, 56–59 SLA Architects
60 Jaime Navarro Soto
62–65 Phillip Johnson Landscapes
66–67 Carol Casselden
68–69 Nigel Dunnett
72 Alla Olkhovska
75 Diana Yule / Glasshouse
76–77 Alla Olkhovska
78–81 Diana Yule / Glasshouse
82–83 Solitary Gardens & the artist jackie sumell
84 Claire Ratinon
85l Christian Cassiel
85r Claire Ratinon
86 Clare Richardson
88, 89l Asian Pacific Family Club
89r Kurisu LLC
90–93 © Britt Willoughby for Lemon Tree Trust
94–95 Seeds of Resilience
96 Melissa Gardner
98, 99a Omari Taylor for The Orchard Project, UK
99bl, 99br The Orchard Project, London, UK

100 Courtesy Green Guerillas, New York
101–103 Caitlin Atkinson
104–107 Teresa Puppo and Alejandro O'Neill at Campo Sucio
108–109 District Six Forest, Cape Town, South Africa, Courtesy of SUGi
110 Photo Ye Rin Mok
111l Emily Berl / *New York Times* / Redux / eyevine
111r Associated Press / Alamy Stock Photo
114 Eugenie Mercier / Nature Urbaine
116–117 Jean-Pierre Gabriel
118–121 Michael Reynolds
122–123 Caroline Duval
124–125 Jean-Pierre Gabriel
126–127 Reuters / Mohammad Ponir Hossain
128 Frederic Reglain / Alamy Stock Photo
129 Eugenie Mercier / Nature Urbaine
130 Rebecca McMackin
132–135 Eva Nemeth
136–139 Tara Rudd / GROW
140–141 Théo Champagnat
142l Associated Press / Alamy Stock Photo
142r–143 PILAR OLIVARES / Reuters
144 John Little
146 Didier ZYLBERYNG / Alamy Stock Photo
147l Andia / Alamy Stock Photo
147r Andia / Universal Images Group via Getty Images
148–149 Slow Food Africa
150–153 OKI Hiroyuki
154–157 Dr Jigmet Yangchan
160 Derek Teo / Alamy Stock Photo
163 Max Carballo Photography & Fine Arts
164–165 Trapa Trapa Forest, Santiago, Chile, Courtesy of SUGi
166l Sergio Azenha / Alamy Stock Photo
166r Photo Godong / Universal Images Group via Getty Images
167 Peach Pics / Alamy Stock Photo
168–169 Phillip Johnson Landscapes
170–171 Kurisu LLC
172–175 Eva Nemeth
176 Portrait by Jooney Woodward
178–181 Max Carballo Photography & Fine Arts
182l Jiaji Wu
182r Nick Dearden
183 Jooney Woodward
184a Jiaji Wu
184bl Jooney Woodward
184br Jiaji Wu

185 Nick Dearden
186–187 Derek Teo / Alamy Stock Photo
188 Yun Hye Hwang
190–191 Greenfingers Charity
192–195 Mikael Colville-Andersen
196–197 Greenstone Design UK
200 Lottie Matthews
202–203 OKI Hiroyuki
204 Sam Oberter
205 Jaime Alvarez
206–207 Kalpana Arias
208–209 OKI Hiroyuki
210al OKI Hiroyuki
210ar, 210b Trieu Chien
211 OKI Hiroyuki
212–213 © Michael Latz, Latz + Partner
214–217 John Little
218 Caitlin Atkinson
220 Emma Stoner
221l Lottie Matthews
221ar Emma Stoner
221br Lauren Wiig
222 Photo Chris Jung / NurPhoto via Getty Images
223al Photo Anthony Wallace / AFP via Getty Images
223bl Photo Simon Shin / SOPA Images / LightRocket via Getty Images
223r Photo Anthony Wallace / AFP via Getty Images
224, 225l Hana Snow
225r, 226 Dave Watts
227 Hana Snow
228–229 The Newt in Somerset
230–231 Caitlin Atkinson
232 Joya Berrow
234 Elly Lucas / Weleda
235l Selina Voelkel / Weleda
235r Elly Lucas / Weleda
236–239 Kate Stanworth
240–241 Jaime Navarro Soto
242–243 Photography by Yamana Garden
244l Aquipor
244cl Raja Jambulingam / Alamy Stock Photo
244cr Lighttrace Studio / Alamy Stock Photo
244r Aaron Coshaw / Alamy Stock Photo
245l Ingrid Balabanova/Shutterstock
245cl Katerina Richterova / Alamy Stock Photo
245cr Dennis Wegewijs / Alamy Stock Photo
245r GCFitzpatrick Photos / Alamy Stock Photo
246l Pavel IARUNICHEV / Alamy Stock Photo

246cl Citizen of the Planet / Alamy Stock Photo
246cr Thomas Garcia / Alamy Stock Photo
246r dpa picture alliance / Alamy Stock Photo
247l Valery Rizzo / Alamy Stock Photo
247cl Ros Drinkwater / Alamy Stock Photo
247cr Simon Turner / Alamy Stock Photo
247r John Richmond / Alamy Stock Photo
248l Andreas von Einsiedel / Alamy Stock Photo
248cl Zoonar GmbH / Alamy Stock Photo
248cr Rob Walls / Alamy Stock Photo
248r Rudmer Zwerver / Alamy Stock Photo
249 GAP Photos/Robert Mabic

Index

350.org 21

Abu Dhabi 54–5
Africa 111, 148 (see also South Africa)
Africa Kaki Community Garden 148
Aghmad 109
Al Fay Park 54–5
Alla Olkhovska's Garden 76–7
America (see USA)
Andean mountains 49
Apiary Studio 201, 204–5
Apple 97
Appleseed, Johnny 73
Arias, Kalpana 96–7, 202, 207
Ashburton 220
Asia 8, 11, 45, 151, 243
Asian Pacific Family Club 89
Atacama desert 49
Attention Restoration Theory 171
Australia 22, 62–3, 168

Baden-Württemberg 46
Bangladesh 115, 126–7
Barbican Estate 68
Barros, Julio Cesar 142
Bath 132
Batheaston 132
Bedmond 182
Beech Gardens 68–9
Bekker, Karen 228
Bekker, Koos 228
Belgium 116, 124, 233
Berkshire 196
Bilbao, Tatiana 178–9
Biophilia 161
Boeri, Stefano 34–5
Bogata Šuma 116
Bogotá 35, 97
Bordeaux 140
Bosco Verticale 22, 34–5

The Botanic Garden 162, 178–81
Botany of Empire 73
Brahmaputra river 126–7
Braiding Sweetgrass 161
Brazil 142
Britain 10, 177
British Empire 73
Brooklyn 31
Brooklyn Bridge Park 30–1, 131
Brooklyn Museum 131
Brown, Capability 8
Brussels 124
Bruton 228
Burrell, Charlie 38

Café Ohlome 101
California 11, 219, 230
Cameroon 233
Camp Bastion 74
Campo Sucio 104–5
Campo, Mariella Gabriella 237
Canada 6
Cape Town 108–9, 233
Care Not Capital 145
Carioca Gardens 142–3
Carioca, Hortas 142
Chalet de la Forêt 116, 124–5
Champagnat, Théo 140
Changpas Mountain Garden 154–7
Chapple, Horatio 173 (see also **Horatio's Garden**)
Charpenal, Patrick 178–9
Chelsea Australian Garden 22, 62–3
Chelsea Flower Show 63
Cheonggyecheon Stream 222–3
Chicago 37
Chile 21, 49, 164–5
China 202
Christchurch 118
Claire House Children's Hospice 191
Clapton 145
Colombia 61, 97, 225, 233

Colville-Anderson, Mikael 192
Community Food System 126
Contemporary Art Space 105
Copenhagen 56–7, 192
Coppel, Augustine 178–9
Courtauld, Henrietta 86–7
Covent Garden 97
CPG Consultants 186
Cranbrook 79
Croatia 116
Crowthorne 196
Culiacán 162, 178–9
Cycloponics 140

Damson Farm 132
Dartmoor National Park 11
Denmark 56, 192
Derbyshire 234–5
Devalkeneer, Pascal 124
Devon 201, 220–1
Dhont, Erik 124
District Six 108–9
Don, Monty 220
Duisburg 201
Duisburg-Meiderich 212
Duke of Cornwall Spinal Treatment Centre 173
Dunnett, Nigel 22, 68, 176–7
Duval, Caroline 122–3

Earthed Charity 207
East Sutton 74, 79
El Chapo 179
Eliasson, Olafur 179
Elle Decor 228
Elworthy, Bridget 86–7
England 6, 11, 74
Essex 22, 145, 201, 214–5
Estudio Ome 24–5
Europe 61, 73, 129
Exmoor 115, 122–3
Extinction Rebellion 74

Farrell, Marchelle 73
Favignana 237
Ferromex 61, 241
Finley, Ron 74, 110–1, 115
Floating Gardens 126–7
Forest Bathing 162, 166–7

Forest Therapy Society 166
France 128, 140, 202

Ganges 126–7
Gangsta Gardening 110–11, 115
Ganguli, Rowena 98
Garden Cities of Tomorrow 115
Garden of the Month 90–1
Gardener's World 177
Garrett, Fergus 66–7
Gaza 94
Germany 46–7, 212, 234
Gertz, Jean-Noël 140
Giardino dell'Impossibile 236–9
The Glasshouse Botanics 78–81
Glitch 97, 202, 207
Godshall, David 22, 218–9
Google 177
Graham, Dan 179
Grampians National Park 168
Grayson, Kitten 201 (see also **Kitten Grayson**)
Great Dixter House and Gardens 66–7
Green Guerillas 100
Greenfingers Charity Hospice Gardens 190–1
Greenstone Design 196
Grey to Green 52–3, 177
GROW 116, 136–7
guerrilla gardening 10, 74, 100

Hackney 145
Hadspen House 228
Hardy, Pascal 128
Harpur, Charlie 38
Harry Johnson Memorial Garden 168–9
Hawkes, Darren 191
Healing Garden 170–1
Helsinki 131
Hermannshof 46–7
Hertfordshire 37, 182
Hesselein, Hans 204–5
The High Line 42–3
Hilldrop 145, 214–5

Hitchmough, James 38
Ho Chi Minh City 151, 201–2, 208
Holt, Sophie 201, 220–1
Holton, Victoria 173
Horatio's Garden 172–5
Houston 97
Howard, Ebeneezer 115
Hudson Rail Yards 43
The Huntingdon Desert Garden 11
Hwang, Yun Hye 188–9

Impossible Garden (*see* Giardino dell'Impossible)
In Search of a Common Paradise 74
India 233
Industrial Revolution 21
Italy 34, 237

Japan 147, 162, 166
Japanese Ministry of Agriculture, Forestry, and Fisheries 166
Jenkins, Alison 132
Jerusalem 74
Jodhpur 233
Johnson, Ayana Elizabeth 21
Johnson, Phillip 62–3, 168
Jurong East 27
Jurong Lake Gardens 22, 26–9
Just Stop Oil 74

Kampung Admiralty 44–5
Kaplan, Rachel 171
Kaplan, Steven 171
Kashmir 154–5
Keen, Martha 204–5
Kenya 116, 148, 225
Kharkiv 73, 76
Khoi First Nations 74, 233
Khoo Teck Puat Hospital 161, 186–7
Kimmerer, Robin Wall 161
Kirinyaga County 148
Kitten Grayson 224–5
Klein, Naomi 21

Knepp Walled Garden 38–41
Kono Design 147
Korea 123 (*see also* South Korea)
Kritzler, Alberto 25
Kurdistan 90–1
Kurisu International 88, 170
Kurisu, Hoichi 89, 171
Kurisu, Michiko 171
Kyiv 192

Ladakh 154–5
Laindon 214
Laing, Olivia 74
Landschaftspark Duisburg-Nord 212–3
Larsen, Henning 27, 45
Latin American Landscape Architecture Biennial 61
Latz + Partner 201, 212
Latz, Peter 213
Lemon Tree Trust 90–1
Let Your Garden Grow Wild 131
Li, Qing 166
Little Harbour Children's Hospice 191
Little, John 22, 144–5, 201, 214–5
Living Planet Index (LPI) 21
Living Planet Report 31
Lloyd, Christopher 66–7
London 68, 74, 116, 136–7, 177, 233
Long, Richard 179
Los Angeles (LA) 74, 110–1, 115, 201, 219
Lydon, John 21
Lyon 140

Malaysia 115
Manguinhos 115, 142
Manhattan 43
Manilla 22
Map of Hope 87
Mapuche 164
Mauritius 73
Mayor Giuliani 43
McKibben, Bill 21

McMackin, Rebecca 130–1
Meatpacking District 43
Medellín 61
Medina, Vincent 101
Mediterranean 49, 237
Mekong river 151
Melbourne 168
Mexican Airways 179
Mexican Society of Landscape Architects (SAPMX) 61
Mexico 24, 61, 162, 178–9, 241
Mexico City 61, 241
MIA Design Studio 201–2, 208
Miami 22
Michael Van Valkenburgh Associates 31
Middle Ages 162
Middle East 28
Milan 22, 34–5
Millstone, Carina 98
Ministry of Health (Singapore) 187
Miyawaki (forestry method) 74, 109, 233
Montevideo 105
Montreal 6
Museum Garden 230–1
Mutitu 148

National Nature Reserves 6
Nature Urbaine 116, 128–9
Nazal, Ximena 21, 49
New Delhi 100
New York 22, 31, 37, 42–3, 74, 100, 233
New Zealand 116, 118
The Newt 228–9
Nordic Therapy Garden 192–5
Northiam 66
Nowadays 96–7, 207

Oare Valley 122–3
Occupy 74
Okasha, Bisan 94
Olinda 22, 62–3
Oliver, Jamie 116, 137
Oliver, Mary 73

Olkhovska, Alla 73, 76–7
The Orchard Project 98–9
Oregon 74, 88, 170
Oregon State Penitentiary Garden 88–9
Organic Research Centre 87
Orozco, Gabriel 179
Oudolf, Piet 42–3
O'Neill, Alejandro 105

Pamela Barnet Centre 196–7
Pape, Becky 171
Paris 10, 115–6, 128–9, 140
Parque Lineal 240–1
Pasona 147
Pasona Urban Farm 146–7
Peauroi, Alain 219
Philadelphia 131, 201, 204–5
Piazza Metallica 213
Pigment 201, 220–1
Pitch Studios 207
Potts, Hadyn 122–3
Puppo, Teresa 105

Queen Elizabeth II 177

Ratinon, Claire 73, 85
Reynolds, Michael 118
Riker's Island 37
Rio de Janeiro 115, 142
Rionda, Fernanda 60–1, 241
RMJM 186
Roimata Food Commons 116, 118–21
The Root Project 122–3
Roy, Arundhati 8
The Ruins 24–5

Saigon (*see* Ho Chi Minh City)
Salem 88
SALT (Solidarity Across Land Trades) 84–5
Samaritan Lebanon Community Hospital 170–1
San Francisco 74, 101, 219, 233
San Marino 11
Santiago 164, 189

Schmidt, Cassian 46–7
Schwäbisch-Gmünd 234
Seeds of Resilience 94–5
Seo-Ahn Total Landscape
    222
Seoul 222–3
Serge Hill Project 37, 182
Sex Pistols 21
Sheffield 22, 52–3, 176–7
Shipley 38
Siberia 77
Sicily 237
Sinaloa Cartel 179
Singapore 22, 27, 45, 161,
    186–9
Sites of Special Scientific
    Interest 67
Skin Food 235
Sky House 201–2, 208–11
SLA Architects 54–7
Slow Food International 148
Snow, Lalage 74
Social and Therapeutic
    Horticulture 37
**Solitary Gardens Project
    82–3**
Somerset 132, 224–5, 228
Somerset House 87
Souter-Brown, Gayle 197
South Africa 49, 74, 108–9, 228
South Korea 222 3
Space Barn 204–5
Sparkes, Joshua 123
St Austell 191
Stalin 77
Stanmore 173
Steiner, Rudolf 235
Sterland, Jayn 235
Stove, Kali Hamerton 79
Stuart-Smith, Sue 36–7, 182
Stuart-Smith, Tom 38, 173, 182
Subramaniam, Banu 73
SUGi 108–9, 164–5, 232–3
sumell, jackie 82–3
Sussex 38, 66, 73
Sweden 192
Symbiótica 164–5
Sótero del Río Hospital 165

Tager Home 196–7
Taipei 8, 10, 35, 115, 201, 242–3
Tarng, Yan-Han 201, 242–3
Tatiana Bilbao Estudio 178
Taylor, Amos 100
Temuco 165
Terremoto 74, 101, 201,
    218–9, 230
Texas 6, 97
*This Changes Everything:
    Capitalism vs. the Climate* 21
Thrive (charity) 37
Thu Duc 151
Tokyo 147, 166
Tomsgårdsvej 56–7
Toronto 8, 35
The Totteridge Academy
    136–7
Tower of London Superbloom
    177
**Trapa Trapa Forest
    Garden 164–5**
Tree, Isabella 6
Tudor, Zac 22, 52–3
Turrell, James 179
Táboas, Sofía 162

Uganda 148
Ukraine 73, 76–7, 192
United Arab Emirates 54
University
    of Copenhagen 192
    of Sheffield 176
    of Singapore 188–9
Uprooting 73
**Urban Farming Office
    150–3**
Uruguay 105
USA 31, 37, 42, 73, 82, 88,
    100–1, 110–1, 161, 170, 204,
    230

Valle de Bravo 24
Valparaiso 21, 49
Van Middelem, Elise 232–3
Victoria 62, 168
Vietnam 151, 201–2, 208
Vivero San Gabriel 48–51
Vo Trung Nghia 151

Wallace, Herman 83
Wardington Manor 87
**Weleda Medicinal Gardens
    234–5**
The Well Gardened Mind 37, 182
What If We Get It Right? 21
Wiggins, Story 101
Willits, Carolyn 191
Wilson, Edward O. 161
Windy City Harvest Youth
    Farm 37
Winstanley, Gerrard 74
Wistman's Wood 11
WOHA Architects 45
World Wildlife Fund (WWF)
    31
Wright, Frank Lloyd 219

**Yamana Permaculture
    Garden 242–3**
Yangchan, Jigmet 154–5
Yangmingshan Mountain 242
Yishun 186

Front cover: Le Chalet de la Forêt, Erik Dhont; Back cover: Floating Gardens, Bangladesh © REUTERS/Mohammad Ponir Hossain

First published in the United Kingdom in 2026 by Thames & Hudson Ltd, 6–24 Britannia Street, London WC1X 9JD

Gardens That Can Save the World © 2026 Thames & Hudson Ltd, London

Foreword © 2026 Isabella Tree
Text by Lottie Delamain © 2026 Lottie Delamain Design

Photographs © 2026 their respective owners as indicated

Design by Studio Noel

EU Authorized Representative: Interart S.A.R.L.
19 rue Charles Auray, 93500 Pantin, Paris, France
productsafety@thameshudson.co.uk
interart.fr

A CIP catalogue record for this book is available from the British Library

ISBN 978-0-500-02874-2
01

Printed and bound in China by RR Donnelley

FSC
www.fsc.org

MIX
Paper | Supporting responsible forestry
FSC® C144853

Be the first to know about our new releases, exclusive content and author events by visiting
thamesandhudson.com
thamesandhudsonusa.com
thamesandhudson.com.au